jQuery 1.4 Reference Guide

A comprehensive exploration of the popular
JavaScript library

Karl Swedberg

Jonathan Chaffer

BIRMINGHAM - MUMBAI

jQuery 1.4 Reference Guide

First published: January 2010

Production Reference: 1190110

Published by Packt Publishing Ltd.
32 Lincoln Road
Olton
Birmingham, B27 6PA, UK.

ISBN 978-1-84951-004-2

www.packtpub.com

Cover Image by Karl Swedberg (karl@englishrules.com)

Credits

Authors

Karl Swedberg

Jonathan Chaffer

Reviewers

Joydip Kanjilal

Dave Methvin

Acquisition Editor

Swapna V. Verlekar

Development Editor

Swapna V. Verlekar

Technical Editor

Tariq Rakhange

Copy Editor

Sneha Kulkarni

Indexer

Hemangini Bari

Production Editorial Manager

Abhijeet Deobhakta

Editorial Team Leader

Mithun Sehgal

Project Team Leader

Lata Basantani

Project Coordinator

Joel Goveya

Proofreader

Chris Smith

Graphics

Nilesh R. Mohite

Production Coordinator

Dolly Dasilva

Cover Work

Dolly Dasilva

About the Authors

Karl Swedberg is a web developer at Fusionary Media in Grand Rapids, Michigan, where he spends much of his time solving problems with JavaScript and implementing design. A member of the jQuery Project Team and an active contributor to the jQuery discussion list, Karl has presented at workshops and conferences, and provided corporate training in Europe and North America.

Before he got hooked on to web development, Karl worked as a copy editor, a high-school English teacher, and a coffee house owner. He gave up his dream of becoming a professional musician in the early 1990s about the same time that he stumbled into a job at Microsoft in Redmond, Washington. He sold his hollow-body Rickenbacker ages ago, but still keeps an acoustic guitar in the basement.

I wish to thank my wife, Sara, for keeping me sane. Thanks also to my two delightful children, Benjamin and Lucia. Jonathan Chaffer has my deepest respect for his programming expertise and my gratitude for his willingness to write this book with me.

Many thanks to John Resig for creating the world's greatest JavaScript library and for fostering an amazing community around it. Thanks also to the folks at Packt Publishing, the technical reviewers of this book, the jQuery Cabal, and the many others who have provided help and inspiration along the way.

Jonathan Chaffer is a member of Rapid Development Group, a web development firm located in Grand Rapids, Michigan. His work there includes overseeing and implementing projects in a wide variety of technologies, with an emphasis on PHP, MySQL, and JavaScript.

In the open source community, Jonathan has been very active in the Drupal CMS project, which has adopted jQuery as its JavaScript framework of choice. He is the creator of the Content Construction Kit, a popular module for managing structured content on Drupal sites. He is responsible for major overhauls of Drupal's menu system and developer API reference.

Jonathan lives in Grand Rapids with his wife, Jennifer.

I would like to thank Jenny for her tireless enthusiasm and support, Karl for the motivation to continue writing when the spirit was weak, and the Ars Technica community for constant inspiration toward technical excellence.

About the Reviewers

Joydip Kanjilal is a Microsoft MVP in ASP.NET, and the author of a number of books on .NET and its related technologies. He has over 12 years of industry experience in IT with more than 6 years in Microsoft .NET and its related technologies. He has authored a lot of articles for some of the most reputable sites such as www.asptoday.com, www.devx.com, www.aspalliance.com, www.aspnetpro.com, www.mcpressonline.com, www.sql-server-performance.com, www.sswug.com, and so on. A lot of these articles have been selected at www.asp.net – Microsoft's official site on ASP.NET. Joydip was also a community credit winner at www.community-credit.com a number of times. Joydip was also selected as MSDN Featured Developer of the Fortnight in November and December, 2008. Joydip has authored the following books:

- *ASP.NET 4.0 Programming* (Mc-Graw Hill Publishing)
- *Entity Framework Tutorial* (Packt Publishing)
- *Pro Sync Framework* (APRESS)
- *Sams Teach Yourself ASP.NET Ajax in 24 Hours* (Sams Publishing)
- *ASP.NET Data Presentation Controls Essentials* (Packt Publishing)

He is currently working as an independent software consultant and author. He has years of experience in designing and architecting solutions for various domains. His technical strengths include C, C++, VC++, Java, C#, Microsoft .NET, AJAX, Design Patterns, SQL Server, Operating Systems, and Computer Architecture. Joydip blogs at http://aspadvice.com/blogs/joydip and spends his time reading books, blogs, and writing books and articles. His hobbies include watching cricket, soccer, and playing chess.

Dave Methvin is the Chief Technology Officer at PC Pitstop and one of the founding partners of the company. He provides technical direction for the PCPitstop. com (`http://www.pcpitstop.com/`) web site and oversees software development.

Before joining PC Pitstop, Dave had an extensive career in computer journalism. He served as an Executive Editor at both *Windows Magazine* and *PC Tech Journal*, co-authored a book on Windows NT networking, and wrote articles for more than two dozen publications. Dave blogs on Windows issues for the InformationWeek (`http://www.informationweek.com`) web site.

Dave holds both a bachelor's and a master's degree in Computer Science from the University of Virginia. He has been active in the jQuery community since 2006 and has written several popular plug-ins such as Splitter.

Table of Contents

Preface

jQuery is a powerful, yet easy-to-use, JavaScript library that helps web developers and designers add dynamic, interactive elements to their sites, smoothing out browser inconsistencies and greatly reducing development time. In *jQuery 1.4 Reference Guide*, you can investigate this library's features in a thorough, accessible format.

This book offers an organized menu of every jQuery method, function, and selector. Entries are accompanied by detailed descriptions and helpful recipes that will assist you in getting the most out of jQuery, and avoiding the pitfalls commonly associated with JavaScript and other client-side languages. If you're still hungry for more, the book shows you how to cook up your own extensions with jQuery's elegant plug-in architecture.

You'll discover the untapped possibilities that jQuery makes available and hone your skills as you return to this guide time and again.

What this book covers

In Chapter 1, *Anatomy of a jQuery Script*, we'll begin by dissecting a working jQuery example. This script will serve as a roadmap for this book, directing you to the chapters containing more information on particular jQuery capabilities.

The heart of the book is a set of reference chapters, which allow you to quickly look up the details of any jQuery method. Chapter 2, *Selector Expressions*, lists every available selector for finding page elements.

Chapter 3, *DOM Traversal Methods*, builds on the previous chapter with a catalog of jQuery methods for finding page elements.

Chapter 4, *DOM Manipulation Methods*, describes every opportunity for inspecting and modifying the HTML structure of a page.

Chapter 5, *Event Methods*, details each event that can be triggered and reacted to by jQuery.

Chapter 6, *Effect Methods*, defines the range of animations built into jQuery, as well as the toolkit available for building your own.

Chapter 7, *AJAX Methods*, lists the ways in which jQuery can initiate and respond to server communication without refreshing the page.

Chapter 8, *Miscellaneous Methods*, covers the remaining capabilities of the jQuery library that don't neatly fit into the other categories.

Chapter 9, *jQuery Properties*, lists properties of the jQuery object that can be inspected for information about the browser environment.

With the catalog of built-in functionality concluded, we'll dive into the extension mechanisms jQuery makes available. Chapter 10, *Plug-in API*, reveals these powerful ways to enhance jQuery's already robust capabilities using a plug-in.

Chapter 11, *Alphabetical Quick Reference*, offers a handy list of all methods and their arguments.

Appendix A, *Online Resources*, provides a handful of informative web sites on a wide range of topics related to jQuery, JavaScript, and web development in general.

Appendix B, *Development Tools*, recommends a number of useful third-party programs and utilities for editing and debugging jQuery code within your personal development environment.

What you need for this book

This book is a reference guide, not a tutorial. As such, prior exposure to the jQuery library will be beneficial in navigating this reference. The book *Learning jQuery 1.3* is well-suited for this purpose.

To understand jQuery concepts, some knowledge of JavaScript is required, and familiarity with HTML and CSS is helpful.

The jQuery library itself can be downloaded from `http://jquery.com/`. The majority of examples in this book require only this library, a text editor, and a web browser. Some AJAX examples require web server software as well, such as Apache, but this requirement is avoided wherever possible.

Who this book is for

This reference is designed for web developers who want a broad, organized view of all that the jQuery library has to offer, or want a quick reference on their desks to refer to for particular details. Basic knowledge of HTML and CSS is required. You should be comfortable with the syntax of JavaScript, and have basic knowledge of jQuery to make best use of this book.

Conventions

In this book, you will find a number of styles of text that distinguish between different kinds of information. Here are some examples of these styles, and an explanation of their meaning.

Code words in text are shown as follows: "The `.removeAttr()` method uses the JavaScript `removeAttribute()` function."

A block of code is set as follows:

```
<ul>
  <li>list item 1</li>
  <li>list item 2</li>
  <li>list item 3</li>
  <li>list item 4</li>
  <li>list item 5</li>
  <li>list item 6</li>
</ul>
```

When we wish to draw your attention to a particular part of a code block, the relevant lines or items are set in bold:

```
<head>
  <meta http-equiv="Content-Type"
    content="text/html; charset=utf-8"/>
  <script src="jquery.js" type="text/javascript"></script>
  <script src="jquery.plug-in.js"
    type="text/javascript"></script>
  <script src="custom.js" type="text/javascript"></script>
  <title>Example</title>
</head>
```

New terms and **important words** are shown in bold. Words that you see on the screen, in menus or dialog boxes for example, appear in the text like this: "After this code executes, clicks on **Trigger the handler** will also display the same message."

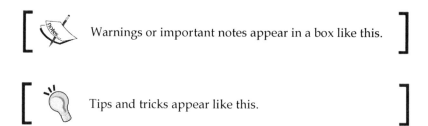

Warnings or important notes appear in a box like this.

Tips and tricks appear like this.

Reader feedback

Feedback from our readers is always welcome. Let us know what you think about this book—what you liked or may have disliked. Reader feedback is important for us to develop titles that you really get the most out of.

To send us general feedback, simply send an email to feedback@packtpub.com, and mention the book title via the subject of your message.

If there is a book that you need and would like to see us publish, please send us a note in the **SUGGEST A TITLE** form on www.packtpub.com or email to suggest@packtpub.com.

If there is a topic that you have expertise in and you are interested in either writing or contributing to a book, see our author guide on www.packtpub.com/authors.

Customer support

Now that you are the proud owner of a Packt book, we have a number of things to help you to get the most from your purchase.

Downloading the example code for the book
Visit http://www.packtpub.com/files/code/0042_Code.zip to directly download the example code.
The downloadable files contain instructions on how to use them.

Errata

Although we have taken every care to ensure the accuracy of our content, mistakes do happen. If you find a mistake in one of our books—maybe a mistake in the text or the code—we would be grateful if you would report this to us. By doing so, you can save other readers from frustration and help us to improve subsequent versions of this book. If you find any errata, please report them by visiting http://www.packtpub.com/support, selecting your book, clicking on the **let us know** link, and entering the details of your errata. Once your errata are verified, your submission will be accepted and the errata will be uploaded on our web site, or added to any list of existing errata, under the Erarata section of that title. Any existing errata can be viewed by selecting your title from http://www.packtpub.com/support.

Piracy

Piracy of copyright material on the Internet is an ongoing problem across all media. At Packt, we take the protection of our copyright and licenses very seriously. If you come across any illegal copies of our works, in any form, on the Internet, please provide us with the location address or web site name immediately so that we can pursue a remedy.

Please contact us at copyright@packtpub.com with a link to the suspected pirated material.

We appreciate your help in protecting our authors, and our ability to bring you valuable content.

Questions

You can contact us at questions@packtpub.com if you are having a problem with any aspect of the book, and we will do our best to address it.

Anatomy of a jQuery Script

A typical jQuery script uses a wide assortment of the methods that the library offers. Selectors, DOM manipulation, event handling, and so forth come into play as required by the task at hand. In order to make the best use of jQuery, it's good to keep in mind the breadth of capabilities it provides.

This book will itemize every method and function found in the jQuery library. As there are so many to sort through, it will be useful to know what the basic categories of methods are and how they come to play within a jQuery script. Here we will see a fully functioning script, and examine how the different aspects of jQuery are utilized in each part of it.

A dynamic table of contents

As an example of jQuery in action, we'll build a small script that dynamically extracts the headings from an HTML document and assembles them into a table of contents for the page. Our table of contents will be nestled on the top-right corner of the page as shown in the following screenshot:

Doctor Dolittle
by Hugh Lofting

▶ Page Contents

Introduction

Puddleby

ONCE upon a time, many years ago when our grandfathers were little children--there was a doctor; and his name was Dolittle-- John Dolittle, M.D. "M.D." means that he was a proper doctor and knew a whole lot.

He lived in a little town called, Puddleby-on-the-Marsh. All the folks, young and old, knew him well by sight. And whenever he walked down the street in his high hat everyone would say, "There goes the Doctor!--He's a clever man." And the dogs and the children would all run up and follow behind him; and even the crows that lived in the church-tower would caw and nod their

We'll have it collapsed initially as shown, but a click will expand it to full height.

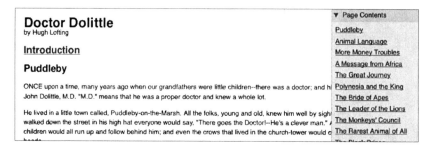

At the same time, we'll add a feature to the main body text. The introduction of the text on the page will not be loaded initially, but when the user clicks on **Introduction**, the intro text will be inserted in place from another file.

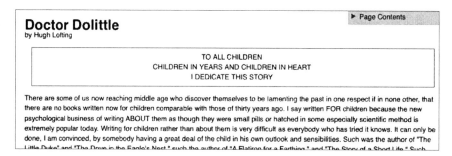

Before we reveal the script that performs these tasks, we should walk through the environment in which the script resides.

Obtaining jQuery

The official jQuery web site (`http://jquery.com/`) is always the most up-to-date resource for code and news related to the library. To get started, we need a copy of jQuery, which can be downloaded right from the front page of the site. Several versions of jQuery may be available at any given moment; the most appropriate for us will be the latest uncompressed version. As of the writing of this book, the latest version of jQuery is 1.4.

No installation is required. To use jQuery, we just need to place it on our site in a web-accessible location. As JavaScript is an interpreted language, there is no compilation or build phase to worry about. Whenever we need a page to have jQuery available, we will simply refer to the file's location from the HTML document with a `<script>` tag as follows:

```
<script src="jquery.js" type="text/javascript"></script>
```

Setting up the HTML document

There are three pieces to most examples of jQuery usage—the HTML document itself, CSS files to style it, and JavaScript files to act on it. For this example, we'll use a page containing the text of a book:

```
<!DOCTYPE html>
<html lang="en">
  <head>
     <meta http-equiv="Content-Type" content="text/html; charset=utf-
     8">
     <title>Doctor Dolittle</title>
     <link rel="stylesheet" href="dolittle.css" type="text/css"
                                        media="screen" />
     <script src="jquery.js" type="text/javascript"></script>
     <script src="dolittle.js" type="text/javascript"></script>
  </head>
  <body>
    <div class="container">
      <h1>Doctor Dolittle</h1>
      <div class="author">by Hugh Lofting</div>
      <div id="introduction">
        <h2><a href="introduction.html">Introduction</a></h2>
      </div>
      <div class="content">
        <h2>Puddleby</h2>
        <p>ONCE upon a time, many years ago when our
           grandfathers were little children--there was a
           doctor; and his name was Dolittle-- John Dolittle,
           M.D.   &quot;M.D.&quot; means that he was a proper
           doctor and knew a whole lot. </p>

           <!-- More text follows... -->
      </div>
    </div>
  </body>
</html>
```

 The actual layout of files on the server does not matter. References from one file to another just need to be adjusted to match the organization we choose. In most examples in this book, we will use relative paths to reference files (`../images/foo.png`) rather than root-relative path (`/images/foo.png`). This will allow the code to run locally without the need for a web server.

Immediately following the standard `<head>` elements, the stylesheet is loaded. Here are the portions of the stylesheet that affect our dynamic elements:

```css
/** =page contents
*****************************************************************/
#page-contents {
  position: absolute;
  text-align: left;
  top: 0;
  right: 0;
  width: 15em;
  border: 1px solid #ccc;
  border-top-width: 0;
  background-color: #e3e3e3;
}
#page-contents a {
  display: block;
  margin: .25em 0;
}
#page-contents a.toggler {
  padding-left: 20px;
  background: url(arrow-right.gif) no-repeat 0 0;
  text-decoration: none;
}
#page-contents a.arrow-down {
  background-image: url(arrow-down.gif);
}
#page-contents div {
  padding: .25em .5em .5em;
  display: none;
  background-color: #efefef;
}

/** =introduction
*****************************************************************/

.dedication {
  margin: 1em;
  text-align: center;
  border: 1px solid #555;
  padding: .5em;
}
```

After the stylesheet is referenced, the JavaScript files are included. It is important that the script tag for the jQuery library be placed *before* the tag for our custom scripts; otherwise, the jQuery framework will not be available when our code attempts to reference it.

 To enable faster rendering of visual elements on the page, some developers prefer to include JavaScript files at the end of the document just before the closing `</body>` tag, so that the JavaScript file is not requested until the majority of the document has been loaded. For more information about this perceived performance boost, see `http://developer.yahoo.com/performance/rules.html#js_bottom`.

Writing the jQuery code

Our custom code will go in the second, currently empty, JavaScript file that we included from the HTML using `<script src="dolittle.js" type="text/javascript"></script>`. Despite how much it accomplishes, the script is fairly short.

```
jQuery.fn.toggleNext = function() {
  this.toggleClass('arrow-down')
    .next().slideToggle('fast');
  return this;
};


$(document).ready(function() {
  $('<div id="page-contents"></div>')
    .prepend('<a class="toggler" href="#">Page Contents</a>')
    .append('<div></div>')
    .prependTo('body');

  $('.content h2').each(function(index) {
    var $chapterTitle = $(this);
    var chapterId = 'chapter-' + (index + 1);
    $chapterTitle.attr('id', chapterId);
    $('<a></a>').text($chapterTitle.text())
      .attr({
        'title': 'Jump to ' + $chapterTitle.text(),
        'href': '#' + chapterId
      })
      .appendTo('#page-contents div');
  });
```

```
$('#page-contents > a.toggler').click(function() {
  $(this).toggleNext();
  return false;
});

$('#introduction > h2 a').click(function() {
  $('#introduction').load(this.href);
  return false;
});
});
```

We now have a dynamic table of contents that brings users to the relevant portion of the text, and an introduction that is loaded on demand.

Script dissection

This script has been chosen specifically because it illustrates the widespread capabilities of the jQuery library. Now that we've seen the code as a whole, we can identify the categories of methods used therein.

 We will not discuss the operation of this script in much detail here, but a similar script is presented as a tutorial on the Learning jQuery blog: http://www.learningjquery.com/2007/06/automatic-page-contents.

Selector expressions

Before we can act on an HTML document, we need to locate the relevant portions. In our script, we sometimes use a simple approach to find an element as follows:

```
$('#introduction')
```

This expression creates a new jQuery object that references the element with the ID introduction. On the other hand, sometimes we require a more intricate selector.

```
$('#introduction > h2 a')
```

Here we produce a jQuery object referring to potentially many elements. With this expression, elements are included if they are anchor tags that are descendants of <h2> elements, which are themselves children of an element with the ID introduction.

These **selector expressions** can be as simple or as complex as we need. Chapter 2, *Selector Expressions*, will enumerate all of the selectors available to us and how they can be combined.

DOM traversal methods

Sometimes we have a jQuery object that references a set of **Document Object Model (DOM)** elements already, but we need to perform an action on a different, related set of elements. In these cases, **DOM traversal** methods are useful. We can see this in part of our script:

```
this.toggleClass('arrow-down')
  .next()
  .slideToggle('fast');
```

Because of the context of this piece of code, the keyword `this` refers to a jQuery object (it often refers to a DOM element, instead). In our case, this jQuery object is in turn pointing to the `toggler` link of the table of contents. The `.toggleClass()` method call manipulates this element. However, the subsequent `.next()` operation changes the element we are working with, so that the following `.slideToggle()` call acts on the `<div>` containing the table of contents rather than its clicked link. The methods that allow us to freely move about the DOM tree like this are listed in Chapter 3, *DOM Traversal Methods*.

DOM manipulation methods

Finding elements is not enough; we want to be able to change them as well. Such changes can be as straightforward as changing a single attribute.

```
$chapterTitle.attr('id', chapterId);
```

Here we modify the ID of the matched element on the fly.

Sometimes the changes are further-reaching:

```
$('<div id="page-contents"></div>')
  .prepend('<a class="toggler" href="#">Page Contents</a>')
  .append('<div></div>')
  .prependTo('body');
```

This part of the script illustrates that the **DOM manipulation** methods can not only alter elements in place but also remove, shuffle, and insert them. These lines add a new link at the beginning of `<div id="page-contents">`, insert another `<div>` container at the end of it, and place the whole thing at the beginning of the document body. Chapter 4, *DOM Manipulation Methods*, will detail these and many more ways to modify the DOM tree.

Event methods

Even when we can modify the page at will, our pages will sit in place, unresponsive. We need **event methods** to react to user input, making our changes at the appropriate time.

```
$('#introduction > h2 a').click(function() {
  $('#introduction').load(this.href);
  return false;
});
```

In this snippet we register a handler that will execute each time the selected link is clicked. The click event is one of the most common ones observed, but there are many others; the jQuery methods that interact with them are discussed in Chapter 5, *Event Methods*.

Chapter 5 also discusses a very special event method, `.ready()`.

```
$(document).ready(function() {
  // ...
});
```

This method allows us to register behavior that will occur immediately when the structure of the DOM is available to our code, even before the images have loaded.

Effect methods

The event methods allow us to react to user input; the **effect methods** let us do so with style. Instead of immediately hiding and showing elements, we can do so with an animation.

```
this.toggleClass('arrow-down')
  .next()
  .slideToggle('fast');
```

This method performs a fast-sliding transition on the element, alternately hiding and showing it with each invocation. The built-in effect methods are described in Chapter 6, *Effect Methods*, as is the way to create new ones.

AJAX methods

Many modern web sites employ techniques to load content when requested without a page refresh; jQuery allows us to accomplish this with ease. The **AJAX methods** initiate these content requests and allow us to monitor their progress.

```
$('#introduction > h2 a').click(function() {
  $('#introduction').load(this.href);
  return false;
});
```

Here the `.load()` method allows us to get another HTML document from the server and insert it in the current document, all with one line of code. This and more sophisticated mechanisms of retrieving information from the server are listed in Chapter 7, *AJAX Methods*.

Miscellaneous methods

Some methods are harder to classify than others. The jQuery library incorporates several **miscellaneous methods** that serve as shorthand for common JavaScript idioms. Even basic tasks like iteration are simplified by jQuery.

```
$('#content h2').each(function(index) {
  // ...
});
```

The `.each()` method seen here steps through the matched elements in turn, performing the enclosed code on all of them. In this case, the method helps us to collect all of the headings on the page so that we can assemble a complete table of contents. More helper functions like this can be found in Chapter 8, *Miscellaneous Methods*.

A number of additional pieces of information are provided by jQuery as properties of its objects. These global and object **properties** are itemized in Chapter 9, *jQuery Properties*.

Plug-in API

We need not confine ourselves to built-in functionality, either. The **plug-in API** that is part of jQuery allows us to augment the capabilities already present with new ones that suit our needs. Even in the small script we've written here, we've found use for a plug-in.

```
jQuery.fn.toggleNext = function() {
  this.toggleClass('arrow-down')
    .next().slideToggle('fast');
  return this;
};
```

This code defines a new `.toggleNext()` jQuery method that slides the following element open and shut. We can now call our new method later when needed.

```
$('#page-contents > a.toggler').click(function() {
  $(this).toggleNext();
  return false;
});
```

Whenever a code could be reused outside the current script, it might do well as a plug-in. Chapter 10, *Plug-in API,* will cover the plug-in API used to build these extensions.

Summary

We've now seen a complete, functional jQuery-powered script. This example, though small, brings a significant amount of interactivity and usability to the page. The script has illustrated the major types of tools offered by jQuery, as well. We've observed how the script finds items in the DOM and changes them as necessary. We've witnessed response to user action, and animation to give feedback to the user after the action. We've even seen how to pull information from the server without a page refresh, and how to teach jQuery brand new tricks in the form of plug-ins.

In the following chapters, we'll be stepping through each function, method, and selector expression in the jQuery library. Each method will be introduced with a summary of its syntax and a list of its parameters and return value. Then we will offer a description, which will provide examples where applicable. For further reading about any method, consult the online resources listed in Appendix A, *Online Resources.* We'll also examine jQuery's plug-in architecture and discuss both how to use plug-ins and how to write our own.

2
Selector Expressions

Each action we perform with jQuery requires a target. For example, in order to hide or show an element on the page, first we must find that element. To do so, we rely on jQuery's **selector expressions**.

Borrowing from CSS 1–3 and then adding its own, jQuery offers a powerful set of tools for matching a set of elements in a document. In this chapter, we'll examine every selector expression that jQuery makes available in turn.

CSS selectors

The following selectors are based on the Cascading Style Sheet specifications (1–3), as outlined by the W3C. For more information about the specifications, visit `http://www.w3.org/Style/CSS/#specs`.

Element (T)

Select all elements that have a tag name of `T`.

Examples

- `$('div')` selects all elements with a tag name of `div` in the document
- `$('em')` selects all elements with a tag name of `em` in the document

Description

JavaScript's `getElementsByTagName()` function is called to return the appropriate elements when this expression is used.

ID (#myid)

Select the unique element with an ID equal to `myid`.

Examples

- `$('#myid')` selects the unique element with `id="myid"`
- `$('p#myid')` selects a single paragraph with an ID of `myid`; in other words, the unique element `<p id="myid">`

Description

Each ID value must be used only once within a document. If more than one element has been assigned the same ID, queries that use that ID will only select the *first* matched element in the DOM. However, this behavior should not be relied on. A document with more than one element using the same ID is invalid.

In our second example, it might not be immediately clear why someone might want to specify a tag name associated with a particular ID, as that `id` value needs to be unique anyway. However, some situations in which parts of the DOM are user-generated may require a more specific expression to avoid false positives. Furthermore, when the same script is run on more than one page, it might be necessary to identify the element ID as the pages could be associating the same ID with different elements. For example, page A might have `<h1 id="title">` while page B has `<h2 id="title">`.

For ID selectors such as the preceding examples, jQuery uses the JavaScript function `getElementById()`, which is extremely efficient. When another selector is attached to the ID selector, like in the second example, jQuery performs an additional check before identifying the element as a match.

As always, remember that as a developer, your time is typically the most valuable resource. Do not focus on optimization of selector speed unless it is clear that performance needs to be improved.

Class (.myclass)

Select all elements that have a class of `myclass`.

Examples

- `$('.myclass')` selects all elements that have a class of `myclass`

- `$('p.myclass')` selects all paragraphs that have a class of `myclass`

- `$('.myclass.otherclass')` selects all elements that have a class of both `myclass` and `otherclass`

Description

For class selectors, jQuery uses JavaScript's native `getElementsByClassName()` function if the browser supports it. Otherwise, it checks the `.className` attribute of each element.

As a CSS selector (for example, in a stylesheet), the multiple-class syntax used in the third example is supported by all modern web browsers, but *not* by Internet Explorer versions 6 and below. This makes the syntax especially handy for applying styles cross-browser through jQuery.

Descendant (E F)

Select all elements matched by F that are descendants of an element matched by E.

Examples

- `$('#container p')` selects all paragraph elements that are descendants of an element that has an ID of `container`

- `$('a img')` selects all `<img>` elements that are descendants of an `<a>` element

Description

Descendants of an element are that element's children, grandchildren, great-grandchildren, and so on. For example, in the following HTML code, the `<img>` element is a descendant of the `<span>`, `<p>`, `<div id="inner">`, and `<div id="container">` elements:

```
<div id="container">
  <div id="inner">
    <p>
      <span><img src="example.jpg" alt="" /></span>
    </p>
  </div>
</div>
```

Child (E > F)

Select all elements matched by F that are children of an element matched by E.

Examples

- `$('li > ul')` selects all `<ul>` elements that are children of an `<li>` element
- `$('.myclass > code')` selects all `<code>` elements that are children of an element with the class `myclass`

Description

As a CSS selector, the child combinator is supported by all modern web browsers including Safari, Mozilla/Firefox, Opera, Chrome, and Internet Explorer 7 and above; but notably *not* by Internet Explorer versions 6 and below. The first example is a handy way of selecting all nested unordered lists (that is, except the top level), and jQuery makes it possible to do this in a cross-browser fashion.

The child combinator (E > F) can be thought of as a more specific form of the descendant combinator (E F) in that it selects only first-level descendants. Therefore, in the following HTML code, the `<img>` element is a child only of the `<span>` element:

```
<div id="container">
  <div id="inner">
    <p>
      <span><img src="example.jpg" alt="" /></span>
    </p>
  </div>
</div>
```

Adjacent sibling (E + F)

Select all elements matched by F that *immediately* follow and have the same parent as an element matched by E.

Examples

- `$('ul + p')` selects all `<p>` elements that immediately follow a sibling `<ul>` element
- `$('#myid + .myclass')` selects the element with `class="myclass"` that immediately follows a sibling element with `id="myid"`

Description

One important point to consider with both the adjacent sibling combinator (E + F) and the general sibling combinator (E ~ F, covered next) is that they only select *siblings*. Consider the following HTML code:

```
<div id="container">
  <ul>
    <li></li>
    <li></li>
  </ul>
  <p>
    <img/>
  </p>
</div>
```

- `$('ul + p')` selects `<p>` because it immediately follows `<ul>` and the two elements share the same parent, `<div id="container">`
- `$('p + img')` selects nothing because `<p>` is one level higher in the DOM tree than `<img>`
- `$('li + img')` selects nothing because even though `<li>` and `<img>` are on the same level in the DOM tree, they do not share the same parent

General sibling (E ~ F)

Select all elements matched by F that follow and have the same parent as an element matched by E.

Examples

- `$('ul ~ p')` selects all `<p>` elements that follow a sibling `<ul>` element
- `$('#myid ~ .myclass')` selects all elements with `class="myclass"` that follow a sibling element with `id="myid"`

Description

One important point to consider with both the adjacent sibling combinator (E + F) and the general sibling combinator (E ~ F) is that they only select *siblings*. The notable difference between the two is their respective reach. While the former reaches only to the *immediately* following sibling element, the latter extends that reach to *all* of the following sibling elements.

Consider the following HTML code:

```
<ul>
  <li class="first"></li>
  <li class="second"></li>
  <li class="third></li>
</ul>
<ul>
  <li class="fourth"></li>
  <li class="fifth"></li>
  <li class="sixth"></li>
</ul>
```

- `$('li.first ~ li')` selects `<li class="second">` and `<li class="third">`

- `$('li.first + li')` selects `<li class="second">`

Multiple expressions (E, F, G)

Select all elements matched by any of the selector expressions E, F, or G.

Examples

- `$('code, em, strong')` selects all `<code>`, `<em>`, and `<strong>` elements

- `$('p strong, .myclass')` selects all `<strong>` elements that are descendants of a `<p>` element, as well as all elements that have a class of `myclass`

Description

This multiple expression combinator is an efficient way to select disparate elements. An alternative to this combinator is the `.add()` method described in Chapter 3, *DOM Traversal Methods*.

Numbered child (:nth-child(n/even/odd/expr))

Select all elements that are the nth child of their parent.

Examples

- `$('li:nth-child(2)')` selects all `<li>` elements that are the second child of their parent

- `$('p:nth-child(odd)')` selects all `<p>` elements that are an odd-numbered child of their parent (first, third, fifth, and so on)

- `$('.myclass:nth-child(3n+2)')` selects all elements with the class `myclass` that are the (3n+2)th child of their parent (second, fifth, eighth, and so on)

Description

As jQuery's implementation of `:nth-child(n)` is strictly derived from the CSS specification, the value of n is "1-based," meaning that the counting starts at 1. However, for all other selector expressions, jQuery follows JavaScript's "0-based" counting. Therefore, given a single `<ul>` containing two `<li>`s, `$('li:nth-child(1)')` selects the first `<li>` while `$('li:eq(1)')` selects the second.

As the two look so similar, the `:nth-child(n)` pseudo-class is easily confused with `:nth(n)`, a synonym for `:eq(n)`. However, as we have just seen, the two can result in dramatically different matched elements. With `:nth-child(n)`, all children are counted, regardless of what they are, and the specified element is selected only if it matches the selector attached to the pseudo-class. With `:nth(n)`, only the selector attached to the pseudo-class is counted, not limited to children of any other element, and the nth one is selected. To demonstrate this distinction, let's examine the results of a few selector expressions given the following HTML code:

```
<div>
  <h2></h2>
  <p></p>
  <h2></h2>
  <p></p>
  <p></p>
</div>
```

- `$('p:nth(1)')` selects the second `<p>` because numbering for `:nth(n)` starts with 0

- `$('p:nth-child(1)')` selects nothing because there is no `<p>` element that is the first child of its parent

- `$('p:nth(2)')` selects the third `<p>`

- `$('p:nth-child(2)')` selects the first `<p>` because it is the second child of its parent

In addition to taking an integer, `:nth-child(n)` can take `even` or `odd`. This makes it especially useful for table-row striping solutions when more than one table appears in a document. Again, given the preceding HTML snippet:

- `$('p:nth-child(even)')` selects the first and third `<p>` because they are children 2 and 4 (both even numbers) of their parent

The third example selector illustrates the most complicated usage of `:nth-child()`. When a simple mathematical expression of the form `an+b` is provided with integers substituted for `a` and `b`, `:nth-child()` selects the elements whose positions in the list of children are equal to `an+b` for some integer value of `n`.

Further description of this unusual usage can be found in the W3C CSS specification at `http://www.w3.org/TR/css3-selectors/#nth-child-pseudo`.

First child (:first-child)

Select all elements that are the first child of their parent element.

Examples

- `$('li:first-child')` selects all `<li>` elements that are the first child of their parent element

- `$(.myclass:first-child')` selects all elements with the class `myclass` that are the first child of their parent element

Description

The `:first-child` pseudo-class is shorthand for `:nth-child(1)`.
For more information on `:X-child` pseudo-classes, see the *Description* for the *Numbered child* selector.

Last child (:last-child)

Select all elements that are the last child of their parent element.

Examples

- `$('li:last-child')` selects all `<li>` elements that are the last child of their parent element

- `$(.myclass:last-child')` selects all elements with the class `myclass` that are the last child of their parent element

Description

For more information on :x-child pseudo-classes, see the *Description* for the *Numbered child* selector.

Only child (:only-child)

Select all elements that are the only child of their parent element.

Examples

- $(':only-child') selects all elements in the document that are the only child of their parent element
- $('code:only-child') selects all <code> elements that are the only child of their parent element

Not (:not(E))

Select all elements that do not match the selector expression E.

Examples

- $(':not(.myclass)') selects all elements in the document that do not have the class myclass
- $('li:not(:last-child)') selects all <li> elements that are not the last child of their parent elements

Empty (:empty)

Select all elements that have no children (including text nodes).

Examples

- $(':empty') selects all elements in the document that have no children
- $('p:empty') selects all <p> elements that have no children

Description

One important thing to note with :empty (and :parent) is that *child elements include text nodes*.

The W3C recommends that the <p> element should have at least one child node, even if that child is merely text (see http://www.w3.org/TR/html401/struct/text.html#edef-P). On the other hand, some other elements are empty (that is, have no children) by definition; for example, <input>, <img>, <br>, and <hr>.

Universal (*)

Select all elements.

Examples

- `$('*')` selects all elements in the document
- `$('p > *')` selects all elements that are children of a paragraph element

Description

The `universal` selector is especially useful when combined with other expressions to form a more specific selector expression.

Attribute selectors

The CSS specification also allows elements to be identified by their attributes. While not widely supported by browsers for the purpose of styling documents, these attribute selectors are highly useful and jQuery allows us to employ them regardless of the browser being used.

When using any of the following attribute selectors, we should account for attributes that have multiple, space-separated values. As these selectors see attribute values as a single string, `$('a[rel=nofollow]')`; for example, will select `<a rel="nofollow" href="example.html">Some text</a>` but *not* `<a rel="nofollow self" href="example.html">Some text</a>`.

Attribute values in selector expressions can be written as bare words or surrounded by quotation marks. Therefore, the following variations are equally correct:

- Bare words: `$('a[rel=nofollow self]')`
- Double quotes inside single quotes: `$('a[rel="nofollow self"]')`
- Single quotes inside double quotes: `$("a[rel='nofollow self']")`
- Escaped single quotes inside single quotes: `$('a[rel=\'nofollow self\']')`
- Escaped double quotes inside double quotes: `$("a[rel=\"nofollow self\"]")`

The variation we choose is generally a matter of style or convenience. The authors choose to omit quotation marks in this context for clarity, and the examples that follow reflect this preference.

Attribute ([foo])

Select all elements that have the `foo` attribute, with any value.

Examples

- `$('[rel]')` selects all elements that have a `rel` attribute
- `$('.myclass[style]')` selects all elements with the class `myclass` that have a `style` attribute

Attribute equals ([foo=bar])

Select all elements that have the `foo` attribute with a value exactly equal to `bar`.

Examples

- `$('[name=myname]')` selects all elements that have a `name` value exactly equal to `myname`
- `$('a[rel=nofollow]')` selects all `<a>` elements that have a `rel` value exactly equal to `nofollow`

Description

For more information on this attribute selector, see the introduction to *Attribute selectors*.

Attribute does not equal ([foo!=bar])

Select all elements that do *not* have the `foo` attribute, or have a `foo` attribute but with a value other than `bar`.

Examples

- `$('a[rel!=nofollow]')` selects all `<a>` elements that either have no `rel` attribute, or have one with a value other than `nofollow`
- `$('input[name!=myname]')` selects all `<input>` elements that either have no `name` attribute, or have one with a value other than `myname`

Description

As these selectors see attribute values as a single string, the first example *will* select `<a rel="nofollow self" href="example.htm">Some text</a>`. Consider the *Attribute contains word* selector for alternatives to this behavior.

Attribute begins with ([foo^=bar])

Select all elements that have the `foo` attribute with a value *beginning* exactly with the string `bar`.

Examples

- `$('[id^=hello]')` selects all elements that have an ID beginning with `hello`

- `$('input[name^=my]')` selects all `<input>` elements that have a `name` value beginning with `my`

Description

This selector can be useful for identifying elements in pages produced by server-side frameworks that produce HTML with systematic element IDs.

Attribute ends with ([foo$=bar])

Select all elements that have the `foo` attribute with a value *ending* exactly with the string `bar`.

Examples

- `$('[id$=goodbye]')` selects all elements that have an ID ending with `goodbye`

- `$('input[name$=phone]')` selects all `<input>` elements that have a `name` value ending with `phone`

Attribute contains ([foo*=bar])

Select all elements that have the `foo` attribute with a value *containing* the substring `bar`.

Examples

- `$('[style*=background]')` selects all elements that have a `style` value containing `background`

- `$('a[href*=example.com]')` selects all `<a>` elements that have an `href` value containing `example.com`

Description

This is the most generous of the jQuery attribute selectors that match against a value. It will select an element if the selector's string appears anywhere within the element's attribute value. Therefore, `$('p[class*=my]')` will select `<p class="yourclass myclass">Some text</p>`, `<p class="myclass yourclass">Some text</p>` and `<p class="thisismyclass">Some text</p>`.

Compare this selector with the *Attribute contains word* selector, which is more appropriate in many cases.

Attribute contains word ([foo~=bar])

Select all elements that have the `foo` attribute with a value containing the word `bar`, delimited by spaces.

Examples

- `$('[class~=myclass]')` selects all elements that have the class of `myclass` (and optionally other classes as well).

- `$('a[rel~=nofollow]')` selects all `<a>` elements with a `rel` value including `nofollow`.

Description

This selector matches the test string against each word in the attribute value, where a "word" is defined as a string delimited by whitespace. The selector matches if the test string is exactly equal to any of the words. Thus, the first example is equivalent to `$('.myclass')`.

This selector is similar to the *Attribute contains* selector, but substring matches within a word do not count. Therefore, the second example matches `<a rel="nofollow" href="example.html">Some text</a>` as well as `<a rel="nofollow self" href="example.html">Some text</a>`, but does not match `<a rel="nofollowself" href="example.html">Some text</a>`.

Attribute contains prefix ([foo|=bar])

Select all elements that have the `foo` attribute with a value either equal to `bar`, or beginning with `bar` and a hyphen (-).

Examples

- `$('[id|=hello]')` selects all elements with an ID of `hello` or an ID that begins with `hello-`

- `$('a[hreflang|=en]')` selects all `<a>` elements with an `hreflang` value of `en` or beginning with `en-`

Description

This selector was introduced into the CSS specification to handle language attributes. The second example, for instance, matches `<a href="example.html" hreflang="en">Some text</a>` as well as `<a href="example.html" hreflang="en-UK">Some text</a>`.

Form selectors

The following selectors can be used to access form elements in a variety of states. When using any of the form selectors other than `:input`, providing a tag name as well is recommended (for example, `input:text` rather than `:text`).

- **Form element (:input)**: Select all form elements (`<input>` (all types), `<select>`, `<textarea>`, `<button>`)

- **Text field (:text)**: Select all text fields (`<input type="text">`)

- **Password field (:password)**: Select all password fields (`<input type="password">`)

- **Radio button (:radio)**: Select all radio button fields (`<input type="radio">`)

- **Checkbox (:checkbox)**: Select all checkbox fields (`<input type="checkbox">`)

- **Submit button (:submit)**: Select all submit inputs and button elements (`<input type="submit">`, `<button>`)

- **Image button (:image)**: Select all image inputs (`<input type="image">`)

- **Reset button (:reset)**: Select all reset buttons (`<input type="reset">`)

- **Standard button (:button)**: Select all button elements and input elements with a type of `button` (`<button>`, `<input type="button">`)

- **File upload (:file)**: Select all file upload fields (`<input type="file">`)

- **Enabled form element (:enabled)**: Select all form elements that are enabled (that is, they do not have the `disabled` attribute and users can interact with them)

- **Disabled form element (:disabled)**: Select all form elements that are disabled (that is, they have the `disabled` attribute and users cannot interact with them)

- **Checked box (:checked)**: Select all form elements — checkboxes and radio buttons — that are checked

- **Selected option (:selected)**: Select all form elements (effectively, `<option>` elements) that are currently selected

Custom selectors

The following selectors were added to the jQuery library in an attempt to address common DOM traversal needs not met by the CSS specification.

Element at index (:eq(n))

Select the element at index n within the matched set.

Examples

- `$('li:eq(2)')` selects the third `<li>` element
- `$('.myclass:eq(1)')` selects the second element with the class `myclass`

Description

The selector `:nth(n)` exists as a synonym of this selector.

The index-related selector expressions (including this selector and the others that follow) **filter** the set of elements that have matched the expressions that precede them. They narrow the set down based on the order of the elements within this matched set. For example, if elements are first selected with a class selector (`.myclass`) and four elements are returned, these elements are given indices 0 through 3 for the purposes of these selectors.

Note that since JavaScript arrays use 0-based indexing, these selectors reflect that fact. This is why `$('.myclass:eq(1)')` selects the second element in the document with the class `myclass`, rather than the first. In contrast, `:nth-child(n)` uses 1-based indexing to conform to the CSS specification.

Greater than (:gt(n))

Select all elements at an index greater than n within the matched set.

Examples

- `$('li:gt(2)')` selects all `<li>` elements following the third one
- `$('.myclass:gt(1)')` selects all elements with the class `myclass` following the second one

Description

See the *Description* for *Element at index*, for important details regarding the indexing used by this selector.

Less than (:lt(n))

Select all elements at an index less than n within the matched set.

Examples

- `$('li:gt(2)')` selects all `<li>` elements preceding the third one
- `$('.myclass:gt(1)')` selects all elements with the class `myclass` preceding the second one

Description

See the *Description* for *Element at index* for important details regarding the indexing used by this selector.

First (:first)

Select the first element within the matched set.

Examples

- `$('li:first')` selects the first `<li>` element
- `$('.myclass:first')` selects the first element with the class `myclass`

Description

The `:first` pseudo-class is shorthand for `:eq(0)`. It could also be written as `:lt(1)`.

See the *Description* for *Element at index* for important details regarding the indexing used by this selector.

Last (:last)

Select the last element within the matched set.

Examples

- `$('li:last)` selects the last `<li>` element
- `$('.myclass:last)` selects the last element with the class `myclass`

Description

While `:first` has equivalent selectors—`nth(0)` and `eq(0)`—the `:last` pseudo-class is unique in its ability to select only the last element in the set of matched elements.

See the *Description* for *Element at index* for important details regarding the indexing used by this selector.

Even element (:even)

Select all elements with an even index within the matched set.

Examples

- `$('li:even')` selects the even-indexed elements within the set of `<li>` elements
- `$('.myclass:even')` selects the even-indexed elements within the set of elements that have the class `myclass`

Description

See the *Description* for *Element at index* for important details regarding the indexing used by this selector. In particular, note that the 0-based indexing means that, counter-intuitively, `:even` selects the first element, third element, and so on within the matched set.

Odd element (:odd)

Select all elements with an odd index within the matched set.

Examples

- `$('li:odd')` selects the odd-indexed elements within the set of `<li>` elements

- `$('.myclass:odd')` selects the odd-indexed elements within the set of elements that have the class `myclass`

Description

See the *Description* for *Element at index* for important details regarding the indexing used by this selector. In particular, note that the 0-based indexing means that, counter-intuitively, `:odd` selects the second element, fourth element, and so on within the matched set.

Is parent (:parent)

Select all elements that are the parent of another element, including text nodes.

Examples

- `$(':parent')` selects all elements that are the parent of another element, including text nodes

- `$('td:parent')` selects all `<td>` elements that are the parent of another element, including text nodes

Description

One important thing to note regarding use of `:parent` (and `:empty`) is that *child elements include text nodes*.

The W3C recommends that the `<p>` element have at least one child node, even if that child is merely text (see `http://www.w3.org/TR/html401/struct/text.html#edef-P`). On the other hand, some other elements are empty (that is, have no children) by definition; for example, `<input>`, `<img>`, `<br>`, and `<hr>`.

Contains text (:contains(text))

Select all elements that contain the specified text.

Examples

- `$('p:contains(nothing special)')` selects all `<p>` elements that contain the text `nothing special`

- `$('li:contains(second)')` selects all `<li>` elements that contain the text `second`

Description

The matching text can appear directly within the selected element in any of that element's descendants, or a combination thereof. Therefore, the first example would still select the following paragraph:

```
<p>This paragraph is <span>nothing <strong>special</strong></span></p>
```

As with attribute value selectors, text inside the parentheses of `:contains()` can be written as bare words or surrounded by quotation marks. *The text must have matching case to be selected.*

Contains element (:has(E))

Select all elements that contain an element matching E.

Examples

- `$('p:has(img)')` selects all `<p>` elements that contain an `<img>` element as a descendant

- `$('.myclass:has(#myid)')` selects all elements with the class `myclass` that contain a descendant with ID `myid`

Description

This expression matches an element if an element matched by E exists anywhere among the descendants, and not just the direct children. For example, the first example matches the `<p>` element in the following HTML code:

```
<div id="container">
  <div id="inner">
    <p>
      <span><img src="example.jpg" alt="" /></span>
    </p>
  </div>
</div>
```

Visible (:visible)

Select all elements that are visible.

Examples

- `$('li:visible')` selects all `<li>` elements that are visible
- `$('.myclass:visible')` selects all elements with the class `myclass` that are visible

Description

The `:visible` selector matches items that are currently visible on the page. Rather than relying on the CSS properties assigned to the element, such as its `display` and `visibility`. jQuery determines whether the element is visible by testing its current width and height.

Elements can be considered hidden for several reasons:

- They have a `display` value of `none`
- They are form elements with `type="hidden"`
- Their `width` and `height` are explicitly set to 0
- An ancestor element is hidden, so the element is not shown on the page

If the element satisfies any of these conditions, it will not be matched by the `:visible` selector.

Hidden (:hidden)

Select all elements that are hidden.

Examples

- `$('li:hidden')` selects all `<li>` elements that are hidden
- `$('.myclass:hidden')` selects all elements with the class `myclass` that are hidden

Description

The `:hidden` selector matches items that are currently hidden on the page. For details on how this determination is made, see the *Description* for *:visible*.

Header element (:header)

Select all elements that are headers, such as `<h1>` or `<h2>`.

Examples

- `$(':header')` selects all header elements
- `$('.myclass:header')` selects all header elements with the class `myclass`

Currently animating (:animated)

Select all elements that are in the progress of an animation at the time the selector is run.

Examples

- `$(':animated')` selects all elements that are currently animating
- `$('.myclass:animated')` selects all elements with the class `myclass` that are currently animating

3
DOM Traversal Methods

In addition to the selector expressions described in Chapter 2, *Selector Expressions*, jQuery has a variety of **DOM traversal methods** that help us select elements in a document. These methods offer a great deal of flexibility, even allowing us to act upon multiple sets of elements in a single chain as follows:

```
$('div.section').addClass('lit').eq(1).addClass('profound');
```

At times, the choice between a selector expression and a corresponding DOM traversal method is simply a matter of taste. However, there is no doubt that the combined set of expressions and methods makes for an extremely powerful toolset for acting on any part of the document we desire.

The jQuery function

The following function underpins the entire jQuery library. It serves as an "object factory," which allows us to create the jQuery objects that all of the other methods are attached to. The function is named `jQuery()`, but as with all uses of that identifier throughout the library, we typically use the alias `$()` instead.

$()

Create a new jQuery object matching elements in the DOM.
```
$(selector[, context])
$(element)
$(elementArray)
$(object)
$(html)
```

Parameters (first version)

- `selector`: A string containing a selector expression
- `context` (optional): The portion of the DOM tree within which to search

Parameters (second version)

- `element`: A DOM element to wrap in a jQuery object

Parameters (third version)

- `elementArray`: An array containing a set of DOM elements to wrap in a jQuery object

Parameters (fourth version)

- `object`: An existing jQuery object to clone

Parameters (fifth version)

- `html`: A string containing an HTML snippet describing new DOM elements to create

Return value

The newly constructed jQuery object.

Description

In the first formulation of this function, `$()` searches through the DOM for any elements that match the provided selector and creates a new jQuery object that references these elements.

```
$('div.foo');
```

In Chapter 2, *Selector Expressions*, we explored the range of selector expressions that can be used within this string.

Selector context

By default, selectors perform their searches within the DOM starting at the document root. However, an alternative context can be given for the search by using the optional second parameter to the `$()` function. For example, if we wish to do a search for an element within a callback function, we can restrict that search like this:

```
$('div.foo').click(function() {
  $('span', this).addClass('bar');
});
```

As we've restricted the `span` selector to the context of `this`, only spans within the clicked element will get the additional class.

Internally, selector context is implemented with the `.find()` method, so `$('span', this)` is equivalent to `$(this).find('span')`.

Using DOM elements

The second and third formulations of this function allow us to create a jQuery object using a DOM element(s) that we have already found in some other way. A common use of this facility is to call jQuery methods on an element that has been passed to a callback function through the `this` keyword.

```
$('div.foo').click(function() {
  $(this).slideUp();
});
```

This example causes elements to hide with a sliding animation when clicked. Because the handler receives the clicked item in the `this` keyword as a bare DOM element, the element must be wrapped in a jQuery object before we can call jQuery methods on it.

When XML data is returned from an AJAX call, we can use the `$()` function to wrap it in a jQuery object that we can easily work with. Once this is done, we can retrieve individual elements of the XML structure using `.find()` and other DOM traversal methods.

Cloning jQuery objects

When a jQuery object is passed as a parameter to the `$()` function, a clone of the object is created. This new jQuery object references the same DOM elements as the initial one.

Creating new elements

If a string is passed as the parameter to `$()`, jQuery examines the string to see if it looks like HTML. If not, the string is interpreted as a selector expression, as previously explained. However, if the string appears to be an HTML snippet, jQuery attempts to create new DOM elements as described by the HTML. Then a jQuery object that refers to these elements is created and returned. We can perform any of the usual jQuery methods on this object:

```
$('<p>My <em>new</em> paragraph</p>').appendTo('body');
```

When the parameter has multiple tags in it, as it does in this example, the actual creation of the elements is handled by the browser's `innerHTML` mechanism. Specifically, jQuery creates a new `<div>` element and sets the `innerHTML` property of the element to the HTML snippet that was passed in. When the parameter has a single tag, such as `$('<img />')` or `$('<a>hello</a>')`, jQuery creates the element using the native JavaScript `createElement()` function.

To ensure cross-platform compatibility, the snippet must be well formed. Tags that can contain other elements should be paired with a closing tag as follows:

```
$('<a></a>');
```

Alternatively, jQuery allows XML-like tag syntax (with or without a space before the slash) such as this:

```
$('<a/>');
```

Tags that cannot contain elements may or may not be quick-closed.

```
$('<img />');
$('<input>');
```

Filtering methods

These methods remove elements from the set matched by a jQuery object.

.filter()

> Reduce the set of matched elements to those that match the selector or pass the function's test.
>
> ```
> .filter(selector)
> .filter(function)
> ```

Parameters (first version)

- `selector`: A string containing a selector expression to match elements against

Parameters (second version)

- `function`: A function used as a test for each element in the set

Return value

The new jQuery object.

Description

Given a jQuery object that represents a set of DOM elements, the `.filter()` method constructs a new jQuery object from a subset of the matching elements. The supplied selector is tested against each element; all elements matching the selector will be included in the result.

Consider a page with a simple list as follows:

```
<ul>
  <li>list item 1</li>
  <li>list item 2</li>
  <li>list item 3</li>
  <li>list item 4</li>
  <li>list item 5</li>
  <li>list item 6</li>
</ul>
```

We can apply this method to the set of list items like this:

```
$('li').filter(':even').css('background-color', 'red');
```

The result of this call is a red background for the items 1, 3, and 5, as they match the selector. (Recall that `:even` and `:odd` use 0-based indexing.)

Using a filter function

The second form of this method allows us to filter elements against a function rather than a selector. If the function returns `true` for an element, the element will be included in the filtered set; otherwise, it will be excluded. Suppose we have a somewhat more involved HTML snippet as follows:

```
<ul>
  <li><strong>list</strong> item 1 -
    one strong tag</li>
  <li><strong>list</strong> item <strong>2</strong> -
    two <span>strong tags</span></li>
  <li>list item 3</li>
  <li>list item 4</li>
  <li>list item 5</li>
  <li>list item 6</li>
</ul>
```

In such a case, we can select the list items and then filter them based on their contents:

```
$('li').filter(function(index) {
    return $('strong', this).length == 1;
}).css('background-color', 'red');
```

This code will alter only the first item in the list as it contains exactly one `<strong>` tag. Within the filter function, `this` refers to each DOM element in turn. The parameter passed to the function tells us the index of that DOM element within the set matched by the jQuery object.

We can also take advantage of the `index` parameter passed through the function, which indicates the 0-based position of the element within the unfiltered set of the matched elements.

```
$('li').filter(function(index) {
    return index % 3 == 2;
}).css('background-color', 'red');
```

This alteration to the code will cause items 3 and 6 to be highlighted, as it uses the modulus operator (`%`) to select every item with an `index` value that, when divided by 3, has a remainder of 2.

.not()

Remove elements from the set of matched elements.

```
.not(selector)
.not(elements)
.not(function)
```

Parameters (first version)

- `selector`: A string containing a selector expression to match elements against

Parameters (second version)

- `elements`: One or more DOM elements to remove from the matched set

Parameters (third version)

- `function`: A function used as a test for each element in the set

Return value

The new jQuery object.

Description

Given a jQuery object that represents a set of DOM elements, the `.not()` method constructs a new jQuery object from a subset of the matching elements. The supplied selector is tested against each element; the elements that don't match the selector will be included in the result.

Consider a page with a simple list as follows:

```
<ul>
  <li>list item 1</li>
  <li>list item 2</li>
  <li>list item 3</li>
  <li>list item 4</li>
  <li>list item 5</li>
</ul>
```

We can apply this method to the set of list items.

```
$('li').not(':even').css('background-color', 'red');
```

The result of this call is a red background for items 2 and 4, as they do not match the selector. (Recall that `:even` and `:odd` use 0-based indexing.)

Removing specific elements

The second version of the `.not()` method allows us to remove elements from the matched set, assuming we have found those elements previously by some other means. For example, suppose our list had an ID applied to one of its items as follows:

```
<ul>
  <li>list item 1</li>
  <li>list item 2</li>
  <li id="notli">list item 3</li>
  <li>list item 4</li>
  <li>list item 5</li>
</ul>
```

We can fetch the third item in the list using the native JavaScript `getElementById()` function, and then remove it from a jQuery object.

```
$('li').not(document.getElementById('notli'))
  .css('background-color', 'red');
```

This statement changes the color of items 1, 2, 4, and 5. We could have accomplished the same thing with a simpler jQuery expression, but this technique can be useful when, for example, other libraries provide references to plain DOM nodes.

As of jQuery 1.4, the .not() method can take a function as its argument in the same way that .filter() does. Elements for which the function returns true are excluded from the filtered set; all other elements are included.

.has()

> Reduce the set of matched elements to those that have a descendant that matches the selector.
>
>   .has(selector)

Parameters

- selector: A string containing a selector expression to match elements against

Return value

The new jQuery object.

Description

Given a jQuery object that represents a set of DOM elements, the .has() method constructs a new jQuery object from a subset of the matching elements. The supplied selector is tested against the descendants of the matching elements; the element will be included in the result if any of its descendant elements matches the selector.

Consider a page with a nested list as follows:

```
<ul>
  <li>list item 1</li>
  <li>list item 2
    <ul>
      <li>list item 2-a</li>
      <li>list item 2-b</li>
    </ul>
  </li>
  <li>list item 3</li>
  <li>list item 4</li>
</ul>
```

We can apply this method to the set of list items as follows:

```
$('li').has('ul').css('background-color', 'red');
```

The result of this call is a red background for item 2, as it is the only `<li>` that has a `<ul>` among its descendants.

.eq()

Reduce the set of matched elements to the one at the specified index.

```
.eq(index)
```

Parameters

- `index`: An integer indicating the 0-based position of the element

Return value

The new jQuery object.

Description

Given a jQuery object that represents a set of DOM elements, the `.eq()` method constructs a new jQuery object from one of the matching elements. The supplied index identifies the position of this element in the set.

Consider a page with a simple list as follows:

```
<ul>
  <li>list item 1</li>
  <li>list item 2</li>
  <li>list item 3</li>
  <li>list item 4</li>
  <li>list item 5</li>
</ul>
```

We can apply this method to the set of list items as follows:

```
$('li').eq(2).css('background-color', 'red');
```

The result of this call is a red background for item 3. Note that the supplied index is 0-based, and refers to the position of the element within the jQuery object, not within the DOM tree.

If a negative number is provided, this indicates a position starting from the end of the set, rather than the beginning. For example:

```
$('li').eq(-2).css('background-color', 'red');
```

The result of this call is a red background for item 4, as it is second from the end of the set.

.first()

Reduce the set of matched elements to the first in the set.
```
.first()
```

Parameters
None

Return value
The new jQuery object.

Description
Given a jQuery object that represents a set of DOM elements, the .first() method constructs a new jQuery object from the first matching element.

Consider a page with a simple list as follows:

```
<ul>
  <li>list item 1</li>
  <li>list item 2</li>
  <li>list item 3</li>
  <li>list item 4</li>
  <li>list item 5</li>
</ul>
```

We can apply this method to the set of list items as follows:

```
$('li').first().css('background-color', 'red');
```

The result of this call is a red background for item 1.

.last()

Reduce the set of matched elements to the final one in the set.

```
.last()
```

Parameters

None

Return value

The new jQuery object.

Description

Given a jQuery object that represents a set of DOM elements, the `.last()` method constructs a new jQuery object from the first matching element.

Consider a page with a simple list as follows:

```
<ul>
  <li>list item 1</li>
  <li>list item 2</li>
  <li>list item 3</li>
  <li>list item 4</li>
  <li>list item 5</li>
</ul>
```

We can apply this method to the set of list items as follows:

```
$('li').last().css('background-color', 'red');
```

The result of this call is a red background for the final list item.

.slice()

Reduce the set of matched elements to a subset specified by a range of indices.

```
.slice(start [, end])
```

Parameters

- `start`: An integer indicating the 0-based position after which the elements are selected
- `end` (optional): An integer indicating the 0-based position before which the elements stop being selected; if omitted, the range continues until the end of the set

Return value

The new jQuery object.

Description

Given a jQuery object that represents a set of DOM elements, the `.slice()` method constructs a new jQuery object from a subset of the matching elements. The supplied `start` index identifies the position of one of the elements in the set. If `end` is omitted, all of the elements after this one will be included in the result.

Consider a page with a simple list as follows:

```
<ul>
   <li>list item 1</li>
   <li>list item 2</li>
   <li>list item 3</li>
   <li>list item 4</li>
   <li>list item 5</li>
</ul>
```

We can apply this method to the set of list items as follows:

```
$('li').slice(2).css('background-color', 'red');
```

The result of this call is a red background for the items 3, 4, and 5. Note that the supplied index is 0-based, and refers to the position of elements within the jQuery object; not within the DOM tree.

The `end` parameter allows us to limit the selected range even further. For example:

```
$('li').slice(2, 4).css('background-color', 'red');
```

Now only items 3 and 4 are selected. The index is once again 0-based. The range extends up to, *but doesn't include*, the specified index.

Negative indices

The jQuery `.slice()` method is patterned after the JavaScript `.slice()` method for arrays. One of the features that it mimics is the ability for negative numbers to be passed as either the `start` or `end` parameter. If a negative number is provided, this indicates a position starting from the end of the set, rather than the beginning. For example:

```
$('li').slice(-2, -1).css('background-color', 'red');
```

This time only the list item 4 turns red, as it is the only item in the range between the second from the end (`-2`) and the first from the end (`-1`).

Tree traversal methods

These methods use the structure of the DOM tree to locate a new set of elements.

.find()

> Get the descendants of each element in the current set of matched elements filtered by a selector.
>
> `.find(selector)`

Parameters

- `selector`: A string containing a selector expression to match elements against

Return value

The new jQuery object.

Description

Given a jQuery object that represents a set of DOM elements, the `.find()` method allows us to search through the descendants of these elements in the DOM tree and construct a new jQuery object from the matching elements. The `.find()` and `.children()` methods are similar, except that the latter only travels a single level down the DOM tree.

The method accepts a selector expression of the same type that we can pass to the `$()` function. The elements will be filtered by testing whether they match this selector.

Consider a page with a basic nested list as follows:

```
<ul class="level-1">
  <li class="item-i">I</li>
  <li class="item-ii">II
    <ul class="level-2">
      <li class="item-a">A</li>
      <li class="item-b">B
        <ul class="level-3">
          <li class="item-1">1</li>
          <li class="item-2">2</li>
          <li class="item-3">3</li>
        </ul>
      </li>
```

```
            <li class="item-c">C</li>
        </ul>
    </li>
    <li class="item-iii">III</li>
</ul>
```

If we begin at item II, we can find list items within it as follows:

```
$('li.item-ii').find('li').css('background-color', 'red');
```

The result of this call is a red background on items A, B, 1, 2, 3, and C. Even though item II matches the selector expression, it is not included in the results; only descendants are considered candidates for the match.

As previously discussed in the section *The jQuery Function*, selector context is implemented with the `.find()` method. Therefore, `$('li.item-ii').find('li')` is equivalent to `$('li', 'li.item-ii')`.

 Unlike in the rest of the tree traversal methods, the selector expression is *required* in a call to `.find()`. If we need to retrieve all of the descendant elements, we can pass in the universal selector `'*'` to accomplish this.

.children()

Get the children of each element in the set of matched elements, optionally filtered by a selector.

```
.children([selector])
```

Parameters

- `selector` (optional): A string containing a selector expression to match elements against

Return value

The new jQuery object.

Description

Given a jQuery object that represents a set of DOM elements, the `.children()` method allows us to search through the immediate children of these elements in the DOM tree and construct a new jQuery object from the matching elements. The `.find()` and `.children()` methods are similar, except that the latter only travels a single level down the DOM tree.

The method optionally accepts a selector expression of the same type that we can pass to the $() function. If the selector is supplied, the elements will be filtered by testing whether they match it.

Consider a page with a basic nested list as follows:

```
<ul class="level-1">
  <li class="item-i">I</li>
  <li class="item-ii">II
    <ul class="level-2">
      <li class="item-a">A</li>
      <li class="item-b">B
        <ul class="level-3">
          <li class="item-1">1</li>
          <li class="item-2">2</li>
          <li class="item-3">3</li>
        </ul>
      </li>
      <li class="item-c">C</li>
    </ul>
  </li>
  <li class="item-iii">III</li>
</ul>
```

If we begin at the level-2 list, we can find its children.

```
$('ul.level-2').children().css('background-color', 'red');
```

The result of this call is a red background behind the items A, B, and C. As we do not supply a selector expression, all of the children are part of the returned jQuery object; if we had supplied one, only the matching items among these three would be included.

.parents()

Get the ancestors of each element in the current set of matched elements, optionally filtered by a selector.

```
.parents([selector])
```

Parameters

- selector (optional): A string containing a selector expression to match elements against

Return value

The new jQuery object.

Description

Given a jQuery object that represents a set of DOM elements, the `.parents()` method allows us to search through the ancestors of these elements in the DOM tree and construct a new jQuery object from the matching elements. The `.parents()` and `.parent()` methods are similar, except that the latter only travels a single level up the DOM tree.

The method optionally accepts a selector expression of the same type that we can pass to the `$()` function. If the selector is supplied, the elements will be filtered by testing whether or not they match it.

Consider a page with a basic nested list as follows:

```
<ul class="level-1">
  <li class="item-i">I</li>
  <li class="item-ii">II
    <ul class="level-2">
      <li class="item-a">A</li>
      <li class="item-b">B
        <ul class="level-3">
          <li class="item-1">1</li>
          <li class="item-2">2</li>
          <li class="item-3">3</li>
        </ul>
      </li>
      <li class="item-c">C</li>
    </ul>
  </li>
  <li class="item-iii">III</li>
</ul>
```

If we begin at item A, we can find its ancestors as follows:

```
$('li.item-a').parents().css('background-color', 'red');
```

The result of this call is a red background for the `level-2` list, the item II, and the `level-1` list (and on up the DOM tree all the way to the document's root element, which is typically `<html>`). As we do not supply a selector expression, all of the ancestors are part of the returned jQuery object. If we had supplied one, only the matching items among these would be included.

.parentsUntil()

> Get the ancestors of each element in the current set of matched elements up to, but not including, the element matched by the selector.
>
> ```
> .parentsUntil(selector)
> ```

Parameters

- `selector`: A string containing a selector expression to indicate where to stop matching ancestor elements

Return value

The new jQuery object.

Description

Given a jQuery object that represents a set of DOM elements, the `.parentsUntil()` method traverses through the ancestors of these elements until it reaches an element matched by the selector passed in the method's argument. The resulting jQuery object contains all of the ancestors up to, but not including, the one matched by the `.parentsUntil()` selector. Consider a page with a basic nested list as follows:

```
<ul class="level-1">
  <li class="item-i">I</li>
  <li class="item-ii">II
    <ul class="level-2">
      <li class="item-a">A</li>
      <li class="item-b">B
        <ul class="level-3">
          <li class="item-1">1</li>
          <li class="item-2">2</li>
          <li class="item-3">3</li>
        </ul>
      </li>
      <li class="item-c">C</li>
    </ul>
  </li>
  <li class="item-iii">III</li>
</ul>
```

If we begin at item A, we can find its ancestors up to but not including `<li class="level-1">` as follows:

```
$('li.item-a').parentsUntil('.level-1')
    .css('background-color', 'red');
```

The result of this call is a red background for the `level-2` list and the item `II`.

If the `.parentsUntil()` selector is not matched, or if no selector is supplied, the returned jQuery object contains all of the previous jQuery object's ancestors. For example, let's say we begin at item A again, but this time we use a selector that is not matched by any of its ancestors:

```
$('li.item-a').parentsUntil('.not-here')
    .css('background-color', 'red');
```

The result of this call is a red `background-color` style applied to the `level-2` list, the item `II`, the `level-1` list, the `<body>` element, and the `<html>` element.

.parent()

> Get the parent of each element in the current set of matched elements, optionally filtered by a selector.
>
> `.parent([selector])`

Parameters

- `selector` (optional): A string containing a selector expression to match elements against

Return value

The new jQuery object.

Description

Given a jQuery object that represents a set of DOM elements, the `.parent()` method allows us to search through the parents of these elements in the DOM tree and construct a new jQuery object from the matching elements. The `.parents()` and `.parent()` methods are similar, except that the latter only travels a single level up the DOM tree.

The method optionally accepts a selector expression of the same type that we can pass to the `$()` function. If the selector is supplied, the elements will be filtered by testing whether they match it.

Consider a page with a basic nested list as follows:

```
<ul class="level-1">
  <li class="item-i">I</li>
  <li class="item-ii">II
    <ul class="level-2">
      <li class="item-a">A</li>
      <li class="item-b">B
        <ul class="level-3">
          <li class="item-1">1</li>
          <li class="item-2">2</li>
          <li class="item-3">3</li>
        </ul>
      </li>
      <li class="item-c">C</li>
    </ul>
  </li>
  <li class="item-iii">III</li>
</ul>
```

If we begin at item A, we can find its parents.

```
$('li.item-a').parent().css('background-color', 'red');
```

The result of this call is a red background for the level-2 list. As we do not supply a selector expression, the parent element is unequivocally included as part of the object. If we had supplied one, the element would be tested for a match before it was included.

.closest()

Get the first element that matches the selector, beginning at the current element and progressing up through the DOM tree.

```
.closest(selector[, context])
```

Parameters

- selector: A string containing a selector expression to match elements against

- context (optional): A DOM element within which a matching element may be found

Return value

The new jQuery object.

Description

Given a jQuery object that represents a set of DOM elements, the `.closest()` method allows us to search through these elements and their ancestors in the DOM tree and construct a new jQuery object from the matching elements.

The `.parents()` and `.closest()` methods are similar in that they both traverse up the DOM tree. The differences between the two, though subtle, are significant:

.closest()	.parents()
Begins with the current element	Begins with the parent element
Travels up the DOM tree until it finds a match for the supplied selector	Travels up the DOM tree to the document's root element, adding each ancestor element to a temporary collection; it then filters that collection based on a selector if one is supplied
The returned jQuery object contains zero or one element	The returned jQuery object contains zero, one, or multiple elements

Consider a page with a basic nested list as follows:

```
<ul id="one" class="level-1">
  <li class="item-i">I</li>
  <li id="ii" class="item-ii">II
    <ul class="level-2">
      <li class="item-a">A</li>
      <li class="item-b">B
        <ul class="level-3">
          <li class="item-1">1</li>
          <li class="item-2">2</li>
          <li class="item-3">3</li>
        </ul>
      </li>
      <li class="item-c">C</li>
    </ul>
  </li>
  <li class="item-iii">III</li>
</ul>
```

Suppose we perform a search for `<ul>` elements starting at item A.

```
$('li.item-a').closest('ul')
  .css('background-color', 'red');
```

This will change the color of the `level-2` `<ul>`, as it is the first `<ul>` encountered when traveling up the DOM tree.

Suppose we search for an `<li>` element instead:

```
$('li.item-a').closest('li')
  .css('background-color', 'red');
```

This will change the color of list item A. The `.closest()` method begins its search with the element itself before progressing up the DOM tree and stops when item A matches the selector.

We can pass in a DOM element as the context within which to search for the closest element.

```
Var listItemII = document.getElementById('ii');
$('li.item-a').closest('ul', listItemII)
  .css('background-color', 'red');
$('li.item-a').closest('#one', listItemII)
  .css('background-color', 'green');
```

This will change the color of the `level-2` `<ul>`, because it is both the first `<ul>` ancestor of list item A and a descendant of list item II. It will not change the color of the `level-1` `<ul>`, however, because it is not a descendant of list item II.

.offsetParent()

Get the closest ancestor element that is positioned.

> `.offsetParent()`

Parameters

None

Return value

The new jQuery object.

Description

Given a jQuery object that represents a set of DOM elements, the `.offsetParent()` method allows us to search through the ancestors of these elements in the DOM tree and construct a new jQuery object wrapped around the closest positioned ancestor. An element is said to be **positioned** if its CSS `position` attribute is `relative`, `absolute`, or `fixed`. This information is useful for calculating offsets for performing animations and placing objects on the page.

Consider a page with a basic nested list with a positioned element as follows:

```
<ul class="level-1">
  <li class="item-i">I</li>
  <li class="item-ii" style="position: relative;">II
    <ul class="level-2">
      <li class="item-a">A</li>
      <li class="item-b">B
        <ul class="level-3">
          <li class="item-1">1</li>
          <li class="item-2">2</li>
          <li class="item-3">3</li>
        </ul>
      </li>
      <li class="item-c">C</li>
    </ul>
  </li>
  <li class="item-iii">III</li>
</ul>
```

If we begin at item A, we can find its positioned ancestor.

```
$('li.item-a').offsetParent().css('background-color', 'red');
```

This will change the color of list item II, which is positioned.

.siblings()

Get the siblings of each element in the set of matched elements, optionally filtered by a selector.

```
.siblings([selector])
```

Parameters

- selector (optional): A string containing a selector expression to match elements against

Return value

The new jQuery object.

Description

Given a jQuery object that represents a set of DOM elements, the .siblings() method allows us to search through the siblings of these elements in the DOM tree and construct a new jQuery object from the matching elements.

The method optionally accepts a selector expression of the same type that we can pass to the $() function. If the selector is supplied, the elements will be filtered by testing whether they match it.

Consider a page with a simple list as follows:

```
<ul>
    <li>list item 1</li>
    <li>list item 2</li>
    <li class="third-item">list item 3</li>
    <li>list item 4</li>
    <li>list item 5</li>
</ul>
```

If we begin at the third item, we can find its siblings as follows:

```
$('li.third-item').siblings().css('background-color', 'red');
```

The result of this call is a red background behind items 1, 2, 4, and 5. As we do not supply a selector expression, all of the siblings are part of the object. If we had supplied one, only the matching items among these four would be included.

The original element is not included among the siblings, which is important to remember when we wish to find all of the elements at a particular level of the DOM tree.

.prev()

Get the immediately preceding sibling of each element in the set of matched elements, optionally filtered by a selector.

```
.prev([selector])
```

Parameters

- selector (optional): A string containing a selector expression to match elements against

Return value

The new jQuery object.

Description

Given a jQuery object that represents a set of DOM elements, the `.prev()` method allows us to search through the predecessors of these elements in the DOM tree and construct a new jQuery object from the matching elements.

The method optionally accepts a selector expression of the same type that we can pass to the `$()` function. If the selector is supplied, the elements will be filtered by testing whether they match it.

Consider a page with a simple list as follows:

```
<ul>
    <li>list item 1</li>
    <li>list item 2</li>
    <li class="third-item">list item 3</li>
    <li>list item 4</li>
    <li>list item 5</li>
</ul>
```

If we begin at the third item, we can find the element that comes just before it.

```
$('li.third-item').prev().css('background-color', 'red');
```

The result of this call is a red background behind item 2. As we do not supply a selector expression, this preceding element is unequivocally included as part of the object. If we had supplied one, the element would be tested for a match before it was included.

.prevAll()

Get all preceding siblings of each element in the set of matched elements, optionally filtered by a selector.

```
.prevAll([selector])
```

Parameters

* `selector` (optional): A string containing a selector expression to match elements against

Return value

The new jQuery object.

Description

Given a jQuery object that represents a set of DOM elements, the `.prevAll()` method allows us to search through the predecessors of these elements in the DOM tree and construct a new jQuery object from the matching elements.

The method optionally accepts a selector expression of the same type that we can pass to the `$()` function. If the selector is supplied, the elements will be filtered by testing whether they match it.

Consider a page with a simple list as follows:

```
<ul>
    <li>list item 1</li>
    <li>list item 2</li>
    <li class="third-item">list item 3</li>
    <li>list item 4</li>
    <li>list item 5</li>
</ul>
```

If we begin at the third item, we can find the elements that come before it.

```
$('li.third-item').prevAll().css('background-color', 'red');
```

The result of this call is a red background behind items 1 and 2. As we do not supply a selector expression, these preceding elements are unequivocally included as part of the object. If we had supplied one, the elements would be tested for a match before they were included.

.prevUntil()

> Get all preceding siblings of each element up to, but not including, the element matched by the selector.
>
> `.prevUntil(selector)`

Parameters

- `selector`: A string containing a selector expression to indicate where to stop matching previous sibling elements

Return value

The new jQuery object.

Description

Given a jQuery object that represents a set of DOM elements, the `.prevUntil()` method allows us to search through the predecessors of these elements in the DOM tree, stopping when it reaches an element matched by the method's argument. The new jQuery object that is returned contains all previous siblings up to, but not including, the one matched by the `.prevUntil()` selector.

If the selector is not matched or is not supplied, all previous siblings will be selected; in these cases it selects the same elements as the `.prevAll()` method does when no filter selector is provided.

Consider a page with a simple definition list as follows:

```
<dl>
  <dt>term 1</dt>
  <dd>definition 1-a</dd>
  <dd>definition 1-b</dd>
  <dd>definition 1-c</dd>
  <dd>definition 1-d</dd>

  <dt id="term-2">term 2</dt>
  <dd>definition 2-a</dd>
  <dd>definition 2-b</dd>
  <dd>definition 2-c</dd>

  <dt>term 3</dt>
  <dd>definition 3-a</dd>
  <dd>definition 3-b</dd>
</dl>
```

If we begin at the second term, we can find the elements that come before it until a preceding `<dt>`.

```
$('#term-2').prevUntil('dt').css('background-color', 'red');
```

The result of this call is a red background behind definitions 1-a, 1-b, 1-c, and 1-d.

.next()

Get the immediately following sibling of each element in the set of matched elements, optionally filtered by a selector.

```
.next([selector])
```

Parameters

- `selector` (optional): A string containing a selector expression to match elements against

Return value

The new jQuery object.

Description

Given a jQuery object that represents a set of DOM elements, the `.next()` method allows us to search through the successors of these elements in the DOM tree and construct a new jQuery object from the matching elements.

The method optionally accepts a selector expression of the same type that we can pass to the `$()` function. If the selector is supplied, the elements will be filtered by testing whether or not they match it.

Consider a page with a simple list as follows:

```
<ul>
    <li>list item 1</li>
    <li>list item 2</li>
    <li class="third-item">list item 3</li>
    <li>list item 4</li>
    <li>list item 5</li>
</ul>
```

If we begin at the `third-item`, we can find the element that comes just after it as follows:

```
$('li.third-item').next().css('background-color', 'red');
```

The result of this call is a red background behind item 4. As we do not supply a selector expression, this following element is unequivocally included as part of the object. If we had supplied one, the element would be tested for a match before it was included.

.nextAll()

> Get all following siblings of each element in the set of matched elements, optionally filtered by a selector.
>
> `.nextAll([selector])`

Parameters

- `selector` (optional): A string containing a selector expression to match elements against

Return value

The new jQuery object.

Description

Given a jQuery object that represents a set of DOM elements, the `.nextAll()` method allows us to search through the successors of these elements in the DOM tree and construct a new jQuery object from the matching elements.

The method optionally accepts a selector expression of the same type that we can pass to the `$()` function. If the selector is supplied, the elements will be filtered by testing whether they match it.

Consider a page with a simple list as follows:

```
<ul>
    <li>list item 1</li>
    <li>list item 2</li>
    <li class="third-item">list item 3</li>
    <li>list item 4</li>
    <li>list item 5</li>
</ul>
```

If we begin at the `third-item`, we can find the elements that come after it.

```
$('li.third-item').nextAll().css('background-color', 'red');
```

The result of this call is a red background behind items 4 and 5. As we do not supply a selector expression, these following elements are unequivocally included as part of the object. If we had supplied one, the elements would be tested for a match before they were included.

.nextUntil()

> Get all following siblings of each element up to, but not including, the element matched by the selector.
>
> `.nextUntil(selector)`

Parameters

- `selector`: A string containing a selector expression to indicate where to stop matching following sibling elements

Return value

The new jQuery object.

Description

Given a jQuery object that represents a set of DOM elements, the `.nextUntil()` method allows us to search through the successive siblings of these elements in the DOM tree, stopping when it reaches an element matched by the method's argument. The new jQuery object that is returned contains all following siblings up to, but not including, the one matched by the `.nextUntil()` selector.

If the selector is not matched or is not supplied, all following siblings will be selected; in these cases it selects the same elements as the `.nextAll()` method does when no filter selector is provided.

Consider a page with a simple definition list as follows:

```
<dl>
  <dt>term 1</dt>
  <dd>definition 1-a</dd>
  <dd>definition 1-b</dd>
  <dd>definition 1-c</dd>
  <dd>definition 1-d</dd>

  <dt id="term-2">term 2</dt>
  <dd>definition 2-a</dd>
  <dd>definition 2-b</dd>
  <dd>definition 2-c</dd>

  <dt>term 3</dt>
  <dd>definition 3-a</dd>
  <dd>definition 3-b</dd>
</dl>
```

If we begin at the second term, we can find the elements that come after it until the next `<dt>`.

```
$('#term-2').nextUntil('dt').css('background-color', 'red');
```

The result of this call is a red background behind definitions 2-a, 2-b, and 2-c.

Miscellaneous traversal methods

These methods provide other mechanisms for manipulating the set of matched DOM elements in a jQuery object.

.add()

Add elements to the set of matched elements.
```
.add(selector[, context])
.add(elements)
.add(html)
```

Parameters (first version)

- selector: A string containing a selector expression to match additional elements against

- context (optional): The portion of the DOM tree within which to search

Parameters (second version)

- elements: One or more elements to add to the set of matched elements

Parameters (third version)

- html: An HTML fragment to add to the set of matched elements

Return value

The new jQuery object.

Description

Given a jQuery object that represents a set of DOM elements, the .add() method constructs a new jQuery object from the union of those elements and the ones passed into the method. The argument to .add() can be pretty much anything that $() accepts, including a jQuery selector expression, references to DOM elements, or an HTML snippet.

Consider a page with a simple list along with a couple paragraphs as follows:

```
<ul>
  <li>list item 1</li>
  <li>list item 2</li>
  <li>list item 3</li>
</ul>
<p>a paragraph</p>
```

```
<div>
  <p>paragraph within a div</p>
</div>
```

We can select the list items and then the paragraphs by using either a selector or a reference to the DOM element itself as the `.add()` method's argument.

```
$('li').add('p').css('background-color', 'red');
```

or

```
$('li').add(document.getElementsByTagName('p')[0])
  .css('background-color', 'red');
```

The result of this call is a red background behind all three list items and two paragraphs.

We can specify a context within which to search for the elements that we wish to add:

```
$('li').add('p', 'div').css('background-color', 'red');
```

Now the result is a red background behind all three list items, but only the second paragraph.

Using an HTML snippet as the `.add()` method's argument (as in the third version), we can create additional elements on the fly and add those elements to the matched set of elements. Let's say, for example, that we want to alter the background of the list items along with a newly created paragraph.

```
$('li').add('<p id="new">new paragraph</p>')
  .css('background-color', 'red');
```

Although the new paragraph has been created and its background color changed, it still does not appear on the page. To place it on the page, we could add one of the **insertion methods** to the chain.

 See Chapter 4, *DOM Manipulation Methods*, for more information about the insertion methods.

.is()

Check the current matched set of elements against a selector and return `true` if at least one of these elements matches the selector.

```
.is(selector)
```

Parameters

- `selector`: A string containing a selector expression to match elements against

Return value

A Boolean indicating whether an element matches the selector.

Description

Unlike the rest of the methods in this chapter, `.is()` does not create a new jQuery object. Instead, it allows us to test the contents of a jQuery object without modification. This is often useful inside callbacks, such as event handlers.

Suppose we have a list, with two of its items containing a child element as follows:

```
<ul>
  <li>list <strong>item 1</strong></li>
  <li><span>list item 2</span></li>
  <li>list item 3</li>
</ul>
```

We can attach a click handler to the `<ul>` element, and then limit the code to be triggered only when a list item itself, not one of its children, is clicked.

```
$('ul').click(function(event) {
  if ($(event.target).is('li') ) {
    $(event.target).css('background-color', 'red');
  }
});
```

Now, when the user clicks on the word **list** in item 1, or anywhere on item 3, the clicked list item will be given a red background. However, when the user clicks on **item 1** in the first item or anywhere in the second item, nothing will happen because in those cases the target of the event would be `<strong>` or `<span>`, respectively.

.end()

> End the most recent filtering operation in the current chain and return the set of matched elements to its previous state.
>
> `.end()`

Parameters

None

Return value

The previous jQuery object.

Description

Most of the methods in this chapter operate on a jQuery object and produce a new one that matches a different set of DOM elements. When this happens, it is as if the new set of elements is pushed onto a **stack** that is maintained inside the object. Each successive filtering method pushes a new element set onto the stack. If we need an older element set, we can use .end() to pop the sets back off of the stack.

Suppose we have a couple short lists on a page as follows:

```
<ul class="first">
    <li class="foo">list item 1</li>
    <li>list item 2</li>
    <li class="bar">list item 3</li>
</ul>
<ul class="second">
    <li class="foo">list item 1</li>
    <li>list item 2</li>
    <li class="bar"></ul>
```

The .end() method is useful primarily when exploiting jQuery's **chaining** properties. When not using chaining, we can usually just call up a previous object by a variable name so that we don't need to manipulate the stack. With .end(), though, we can string all of the method calls together.

```
$('ul.first').find('.foo').css('background-color', 'red')
    .end().find('.bar').css('background-color', 'green');
```

This chain searches for items with the foo class within the first list only and turns their backgrounds red. Then .end() returns the object to its state before the call to .find(). So the second .find() looks for '.bar' inside <ul class="first">, not just inside that list's <li class="foo">, and turns the matching elements' backgrounds green. The net result is that items 1 and 3 of the first list have a colored background, while none of the items from the second list do.

A long jQuery chain can be visualized as a structured code block with filtering methods providing the openings of nested blocks and .end() methods closing them:

```
$('ul.first').find('.foo')
    .css('background-color', 'red')
.end().find('.bar')
    .css('background-color', 'green')
.end();
```

The last `.end()` is unnecessary, as we are discarding the jQuery object immediately thereafter. However, when the code is written in this form, the `.end()` provides visual symmetry and closure, making the program more readable at least in the eyes of some developers.

.andSelf()

> Add the previous set of elements on the stack to the current set.
>
>   .andSelf()

Parameters

None

Return value

The new jQuery object.

Description

As previously described in the *Description* for *.end()*, jQuery objects maintain an internal stack that keeps track of changes to the matched set of elements. When one of the DOM traversal methods is called, the new set of elements is pushed onto the stack. If the previous set of elements is desired as well, `.andSelf()` can help.

Consider a page with a simple list as follows:

```
<ul>
    <li>list item 1</li>
    <li>list item 2</li>
    <li class="third-item">list item 3</li>
    <li>list item 4</li>
    <li>list item 5</li>
</ul>
```

If we begin at the third item, we can find the elements that come after it.

```
$('li.third-item').nextAll().andSelf()
    .css('background-color', 'red');
```

The result of this call is a red background behind items 3, 4 and 5. First, the initial selector locates item 3, initializing the stack with the set containing just this item. The call to `.nextAll()` then pushes the set of items 4 and 5 onto the stack. Finally, the `.andSelf()` invocation merges these two sets together, creating a jQuery object that points to all three items.

.map()

> Pass each element in the current matched set through a function, producing a
> new jQuery object containing the return values.
>
> ```
> .map(callback)
> ```

Parameters

- `callback`: A function object that will be invoked for each element in the
  current set

Return value

The new jQuery object.

Description

The `.map()` method is particularly useful for getting or setting the value of a
collection of elements. Consider a form with a set of checkboxes as follows:

```
<form method="post" action="">
  <fieldset>
    <div>
      <label for="two">2</label>
      <input type="checkbox" value="2" id="two" name="number[]">
    </div>
    <div>
      <label for="four">4</label>
      <input type="checkbox" value="4" id="four" name="number[]">
    </div>
    <div>
      <label for="six">6</label>
      <input type="checkbox" value="6" id="six" name="number[]">
    </div>
    <div>
      <label for="eight">8</label>
      <input type="checkbox" value="8" id="eight" name="number[]">
    </div>
  </fieldset>
</form>
```

We can select all of the checkboxes by setting their checked property to true.

```
$(':checkbox').map(function() {
 return this.checked = true;
});
```

We can get the sum of the values of the checked inputs as follows:

```
var sum = 0;
$(':checked').map(function() {
 return sum += (this.value * 1);
});
```

We can get a comma-separated list of checkbox IDs.

```
$(':checkbox').map(function() {
   return this.id;
}).get().join(',');
```

The result of this call is the `two,four,six,eight` string.

.contents()

> Get the children of each element in the set of matched elements, including text nodes.
>
>   .contents()

Parameters

None

Return value

The new jQuery object.

Description

Given a jQuery object that represents a set of DOM elements, the `.contents()` method allows us to search through the immediate children of these elements in the DOM tree and construct a new jQuery object from the matching elements. The `.contents()` and `.children()` methods are similar, except that the former includes text nodes as well as HTML elements in the resulting jQuery object.

Consider a simple `<div>` with a number of text nodes, each of which is separated by two line break elements (`<br />`) as follows:

```
<div class="container">
   Lorem ipsum dolor sit amet, consectetur adipisicing elit, sed do
eiusmod tempor incididunt ut labore et dolore magna aliqua. <br /><br
/>
   Ut enim ad minim veniam, quis nostrud exercitation ullamco laboris
nisi ut aliquip ex ea commodo consequat.<br /><br />
    Duis aute irure dolor in reprehenderit in voluptate velit esse
cillum dolore eu fugiat nulla pariatur.
    </div>
```

We can employ the `.contents()` method to help convert this block of text into three well-formed paragraphs.

```
$('.container').contents().filter(function() {
   return this.nodeType == 3;
})
   .wrap('<p></p>')
.end()
.filter('br')
   .remove();
```

This code first retrieves the contents of `<div class="container">` and then filters it for text nodes, which are wrapped in paragraph tags. This is accomplished by testing the `.nodeType` property of the element. This DOM property holds a numeric code indicating the node's type — text nodes use the code 3. The contents are again filtered, this time for `<br />` elements, and then these elements are removed.

4
DOM Manipulation Methods

All of the methods in this chapter manipulate the DOM in some manner. A few of them simply change one of the attributes of an element, while others set an element's style properties. Still others modify entire elements (or groups of elements) themselves—inserting, copying, removing, and so on. All of these methods are referred to as **setters**, as they change the values of properties.

A few of these methods such as .attr(), .html(), and .val() also act as **getters**, retrieving information from DOM elements for later use.

General attributes

These methods get and set DOM attributes of elements.

.attr() (getter)

> Get the value of an attribute for the first element in the set of matched elements.
>
>   .attr(attributeName)

Parameters

* attributeName: The name of the attribute to get

Return value

A string containing the attribute value.

Description

It's important to note that the `.attr()` method gets the attribute value for only the *first* element in the matched set. To get the value for each element individually, we need to rely on a looping construct such as jQuery's `.each()` method.

Using jQuery's `.attr()` method to get the value of an element's attribute has two main benefits:

- **Convenience**: It can be called directly on a jQuery object and chained to other jQuery methods.
- **Cross-browser consistency**: Some attributes have inconsistent naming from browser to browser. Furthermore, the values of some attributes are reported inconsistently across browsers, and even across versions of a single browser. The `.attr()` method reduces such inconsistencies.

.attr() (setter)

Set one or more attributes for the set of matched elements.
```
.attr(attributeName, value)
.attr(map)
.attr(attributeName, function)
```

Parameters (first version)

- `attributeName`: The name of the attribute to set
- `value`: A value to set for the attribute

Parameters (second version)

- `map`: A map of attribute-value pairs to set

Parameters (third version)

- `attributeName`: The name of the attribute to set
- `function`: A function returning the value to set

Return value

The jQuery object, for chaining purposes.

Description

The .attr() method is a convenient and powerful way to set the value of attributes, especially when setting multiple attributes or using values returned by a function. Let's consider the following image:

```
<img id="greatphoto" src="brush-seller.jpg"
    alt="brush seller" />
```

Setting a simple attribute

We can change the alt attribute by simply passing the name of the attribute and its new value to the .attr() method.

```
$('#greatphoto').attr('alt', 'Beijing Brush Seller');
```

We can *add* an attribute the same way.

```
$('#greatphoto')
    .attr('title', 'Photo by Kelly Clark');
```

Setting several attributes at once

To change the alt attribute and add the title attribute at the same time, we can pass both sets of names and values into the method at once using a map (JavaScript object literal). Each key-value pair in the map adds or modifies an attribute:

```
$('#greatphoto').attr({
    alt: 'Beijing Brush Seller',
    title: 'photo by Kelly Clark'
});
```

When setting multiple attributes, the quotation marks around attribute names are optional.

Computed attribute values

By using a function to set attributes, we can compute the value based on other properties of the element. For example, we could concatenate a new value with an existing value as follows:

```
$('#greatphoto').attr('title', function() {
    return this.alt + ' - photo by Kelly Clark'
});
```

This use of a function to compute attribute values can be particularly useful when we modify the attributes of multiple elements at once.

.removeAttr()

Remove an attribute from each element in the set of matched elements.

```
.removeAttr(attributeName)
.removeAttr(function)
```

Parameters (first version)

- `attributeName`: An attribute to remove

Parameters (second version)

- `function`: A function returning the attribute to remove

Return value

The jQuery object, for chaining purposes.

Description

The `.removeAttr()` method uses the JavaScript `removeAttribute()` function, but it has the advantage of being able to be called directly on a jQuery object and it accounts for different attribute naming across browsers.

As of jQuery 1.4, the `.removeAttr()` function allows us to indicate the attribute to be removed by passing in a function.

Style properties

These methods get and set CSS-related properties of elements.

.css() (getter)

Get the value of a style property for the first element in the set of matched elements.

```
.css(propertyName)
```

Parameters

- `propertyName`: A CSS property

Return value

A string containing the CSS property value.

Description

The .css() method is a convenient way to get a style property from the first matched element, especially in light of the different ways browsers access most of those properties (the getComputedStyle() method in standards-based browsers versus the currentStyle and runtimeStyle properties in Internet Explorer) and the different terms browsers use for certain properties. For example, Internet Explorer's DOM implementation refers to the float property as styleFloat, while W3C standards-compliant browsers refer to it as cssFloat. The .css() method accounts for such differences, producing the same result no matter which term we use. For example, an element that is floated left will return the left string for each of the following three lines:

- $('div.left').css('float');

- $('div.left').css('cssFloat');

- $('div.left').css('styleFloat');

Also, jQuery can equally interpret the CSS and DOM formatting of multiple-word properties. For example, jQuery understands and returns the correct value for both .css('background-color') and .css('backgroundColor').

.css() (setter)

Set one or more CSS properties for the set of matched elements.

    .css(propertyName, value)
    .css(map)
    .css(propertyName, function)

Parameters (first version)

- propertyName: A CSS property name

- value: A value to set for the property

Parameters (second version)

- map: A map of property-value pairs to set

Parameters (third version)

- propertyName: A CSS property name

- function: A function returning the value to set

Return value

The jQuery object, for chaining purposes.

Description

As with the `.attr()` method, the `.css()` method makes setting properties of elements quick and easy. This method can take either a property name and value as separate parameters, or a single map of key-value pairs (JavaScript object notation).

Also, jQuery can equally interpret the CSS and DOM formatting of multiple-word properties. For example, jQuery understands and returns the correct value for both `.css({'background-color': '#ffe', 'border-left': '5px solid #ccc'})` and `.css({backgroundColor: '#ffe', borderLeft: '5px solid #ccc'})`. Notice that with the DOM notation, quotation marks around the property names are optional. However, with CSS notation they're required due to the hyphen in the name.

As with `.attr()`, `.css()` allows us to pass a function as the property value as follows:

```
$('div.example').css('width', function(index) {
  return index * 50;
});
```

This example sets the widths of the matched elements to incrementally larger values.

.height() (getter)

> Get the current computed height for the first element in the set of matched elements.
>
>   .height()

Parameters

None

Return value

The height of the element in pixels

Description

The difference between `.css('height')` and `.height()` is that the latter returns a unitless pixel value (for example, `400`), while the former returns a value with units intact (for example, `400px`). The `.height()` method is recommended when an element's height needs to be used in a mathematical calculation.

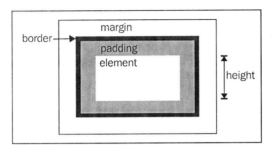

.height() (setter)

Set the CSS height of each element in the set of matched elements.

    .height(value)

Parameters

* `value`: An integer representing the number of pixels, or an integer with an optional unit of measure appended

Return value

The jQuery object, for chaining purposes.

Description

When calling `.height(value)`, the value can be either a string (number and unit) or a number. If only a number is provided for the value, jQuery assumes a pixel unit. However, if a string is provided, any valid CSS measurement may be used for the height (such as `100px`, `50%`, or `auto`). Note that in modern browsers, the CSS height property does not include padding, border, or margin.

.innerHeight()

Get the current computed height for the first element in the set of matched elements, including padding but not border.

        .innerHeight()

Parameters

None

Return value

The height of the element in pixels, including top and bottom padding.

Description

This method is not applicable to window and document objects; for these use .height() instead.

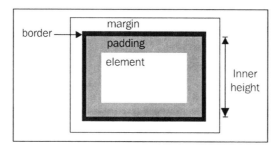

.outerHeight()

Get the current computed height for the first element in the set of matched elements, including padding and border.

        .outerHeight([includeMargin])

Parameters

- `includeMargin`: A Boolean indicating whether to include the element's margin in the calculation

Return value

The height of the element, along with its top and bottom padding, border, and optionally margin, in pixels.

Description

If `includeMargin` is omitted or `false`, the padding and border are included in the calculation; if it's `true`, the margin is also included.

This method is not applicable to `window` and `document` objects, for these use `.height()` instead.

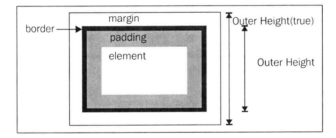

.width() (getter)

Get the current computed width for the first element in the set of matched elements.

        .width()

Parameters

None

Return value

The width of the element in pixels.

Description

The difference between .css(width) and .width() is that the latter returns a unitless pixel value (for example, 400), while the former returns a value with units intact (for example, 400px). The .width() method is recommended when an element's width needs to be used in a mathematical calculation.

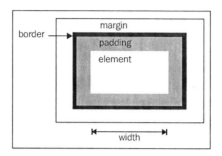

.width() (setter)

Set the CSS width of each element in the set of matched elements.

.width(value)

Parameters

- value: An integer representing the number of pixels, or an integer along with an optional unit of measure appended

Return value

The jQuery object, for chaining purposes.

Description

When calling .width('value'), the value can be either a string (number and unit) or a number. If only a number is provided for the value, jQuery assumes a pixel unit. However, if a string is provided, any valid CSS measurement may be used for the width (such as 100px, 50%, or auto). Note that in modern browsers, the CSS width property does not include padding, border, or margin.

.innerWidth()

Get the current computed width for the first element in the set of matched elements, including padding but not border.

```
.innerWidth()
```

Parameters

None

Return value

The width of the element, including left and right padding, in pixels.

Description

This method is not applicable to `window` and `document` objects, for these use `.width()` instead.

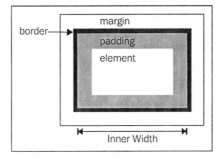

.outerWidth()

Get the current computed width for the first element in the set of matched elements, including padding and border.

```
.outerWidth([includeMargin])
```

Parameters

- `includeMargin`: A Boolean indicating whether to include the element's margin in the calculation

Return value

The width of the element, along with left and right padding, border, and optionally margin, in pixels.

Description

If `includeMargin` is omitted or `false`, the padding and border are included in the calculation; if it's `true`, the margin is also included.

This method is not applicable to `window` and `document` objects; for these use `.width()` instead.

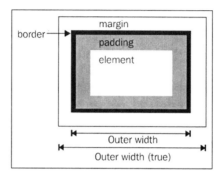

.offset() (getter)

> Get the current coordinates of the first element in the set of matched elements relative to the document.
>
>   .offset()

Parameters

None

Return value

An object containing the properties `top` and `left`.

Description

The .offset() method allows us to retrieve the current position of an element *relative to the document*. Contrast this with .position(), which retrieves the current position *relative to the offset parent*. When positioning a new element on top of an existing one for global manipulation (in particular, for implementing drag-and-drop), .offset() is more useful.

.offset() (setter)

> Set the current coordinates of the first element in the set of matched elements relative to the document.
>
>   .offset(coordinates)

Parameters

- coordinates: An object containing the top and left properties, which are integers indicating the new top and left coordinates for the element

Return value

The jQuery object, for chaining purposes.

Description

The .offset() setter method allows us to reposition an element. The element's position is specified *relative to the document*. If the element's position style property is currently static, it will be set to relative to allow for this repositioning.

.position()

> Get the current coordinates of the first element in the set of matched elements, relative to the offset parent.
>
>   .position()

Parameters

None

Return value

An object containing the properties top and left.

Description

The .position() method allows us to retrieve the current position of an element *relative to the offset parent*. Contrast this with .offset(), which retrieves the current position *relative to the document*. When positioning a new element near another one within the same DOM element, .position() is more useful.

.scrollTop() (getter)

> Get the current vertical position of the scroll bar for the first element in the set of matched elements.
>
> .scrollTop()

Parameters

None

Return value

The vertical scroll position in pixels.

Description

The vertical scroll position is the same as the number of pixels that are hidden from view above the scrollable area. If the scroll bar is at the very top, or if the element is not scrollable, this number will be 0.

.scrollTop() (setter)

> Set the current vertical position of the scroll bar for each of the sets of matched elements.
>
> .scrollTop(value)

Parameters

* value: An integer indicating the new position to set the scroll bar to

Return value

The jQuery object, for chaining purposes.

.scrollLeft() (getter)

Get the current horizontal position of the scroll bar for the first element in the set of matched elements.

```
.scrollLeft()
```

Parameters

None

Return value

The horizontal scroll position in pixels.

Description

The horizontal scroll position is the same as the number of pixels that are hidden from view to the left of the scrollable area. If the scroll bar is at the very left, or if the element is not scrollable, this number will be 0.

.scrollLeft() (setter)

Set the current horizontal position of the scroll bar for each of the set of matched elements.

```
.scrollLeft(value)
```

Parameters

* `value`: An integer indicating the new position to set the scroll bar to

Return value

The jQuery object, for chaining purposes

Class attributes

These methods inspect and manipulate the CSS classes assigned to elements.

.hasClass()

Determine whether any of the matched elements are assigned
the given class.

```
.hasClass(className)
```

Parameters

- `className`: The class name to search for

Return value

A Boolean indicating whether the class is assigned to an element in the set.

Description

Elements may have more than one class assigned to them. In HTML, this is
represented by separating the class names with a space:

```
<div id="mydiv" class="foo bar"></div>
```

The `.hasClass()` method will return `true` if the class is assigned to an element, and
it will also return `true` if any other classes are assigned to it. For example, given the
preceding HTML code, the following will return `true`:

- `$('#mydiv').hasClass('foo')`
- `$('#mydiv').hasClass('bar')`

.addClass()

Add one or more classes to each element in the set of matched elements.

```
.addClass(className)
.addClass(function)
```

Parameters (first version)

- `className`: One or more class names to be added to the class attribute of
each matched element

Parameters (second version)

- `function`: A function returning one or more space-separated class names to
be added

Return value

The jQuery object, for chaining purposes.

Description

It's important to note that this method does not replace a class. It simply adds the class, appending it to any which may already be assigned to the elements.

More than one class may be added at a time, separated by a space, to the set of matched elements.

```
$('p').addClass('myClass yourClass');
```

This method is often used with `.removeClass()` to switch elements' classes from one to another.

```
$('p').removeClass('myClass noClass').addClass('yourClass');
```

Here, the `myClass` and `noClass` classes are removed from all paragraphs; while `yourClass` is added.

As of jQuery 1.4, the `.addClass()` method allows us to set the class name by passing in a function.

```
$('ul li:last').addClass(function() {
  return 'item-' + $(this).index();
});
```

Given an unordered list with five `<li>` elements, this example adds the `item-4` class to the last `<li>`.

.removeClass()

Remove one or all classes from each element in the set of matched elements.
```
.removeClass([className])
.removeClass([function])
```

Parameters (first version)

- `className` (optional): A class name to be removed from the class attribute of each matched element

Parameters (second version)

- `function` (optional): A function returning one or more space-separated class names to be removed

Return value

The jQuery object, for chaining purposes.

Description

If a class name is included as a parameter, then only that class will be removed from the set of matched elements. If no class names are specified in the parameter, all classes will be removed.

More than one class may be removed at a time, separated by a space, from the set of matched elements.

```
$('p').removeClass('myClass yourClass')
```

This method is often used with `.addClass()` to switch elements' classes from one to another.

```
$('p').removeClass('myClass noClass').addClass('yourClass');
```

Here, the `myClass` and `noClass` classes are removed from all paragraphs; while `yourClass` is added.

To replace all existing classes with another class, we can use `.attr('class', 'newClass')` instead.

The `.removeClass()` method allows us to indicate the class to be removed by passing in a function.

```
$('li:last').removeClass(function() {
    return $(this).prev().attr('class');
});
```

This example removes the class name of the penultimate `<li>` from the last `<li>`.

.toggleClass()

Add or remove a class from each element in the set of matched elements, depending on either its presence or the value of the addOrRemove argument.

```
.toggleClass(className)
.toggleClass(className, addOrRemove)
.toggleClass(function[, addOrRemove])
```

Parameters (first version)

- className: A class name to be toggled in the class attribute of each element in the matched set

Parameters (second version)

- className: A class name to be toggled in the class attribute of each element in the matched set

- addOrRemove: A Boolean indicating whether to add or remove the class

Parameters (third version)

- function: A function that returns a class name to be toggled in the class attribute of each element in the matched set

- addOrRemove (optional): A Boolean indicating whether to add or remove the class

Return value

The jQuery object, for chaining purposes.

Description

This method takes one or more class names as its parameter. In the first version, if an element in the matched set of elements already has the class, then it is removed; if an element does not have the class, then it is added. For example, we can apply `.toggleClass()` to a simple `<div>` as follows:

```
<div class="tumble">Some text.</div>
```

The first time we apply `$('div.tumble').toggleClass('bounce')`, we get the following:

```
<div class="tumble bounce">Some text.</div>
```

The second time we apply `$('div.tumble').toggleClass('bounce')`, the `<div>` class is returned to the single `tumble` value as follows:

```
<div class="tumble">Some text.</div>
```

Applying `.toggleClass('bounce spin')` to the same `<div>` alternates between `<div class="tumble bounce spin">` and `<div class="tumble">`.

The second version of `.toggleClass()` uses the second parameter for determining whether the class should be added or removed. If this parameter's value is `true`, then the class is added; if `false`, the class is removed. In essence, the statement:

```
$('#foo').toggleClass(className, addOrRemove);
```

is equivalent to

```
if (addOrRemove) {
  $('#foo').addClass(className);
}
else {
  $('#foo').removeClass(className);
}
```

As of jQuery 1.4, the `.toggleClass()` method allows us to indicate the class name to be toggled by passing in a function.

```
$('div.foo').toggleClass(function() {
  if ($(this).parent().is('.bar') {
    return 'happy';
  } else {
    return 'sad';
  }
});
```

This example will toggle the `happy` class for `<div class="foo">` elements if their parent element has a class of `bar`; otherwise, it will toggle the `sad` class.

DOM replacement

These methods are used to remove content from the DOM and replace it with new content.

.html() (getter)

Get the HTML contents of the first element in the set of matched elements.
```
.html()
```

Parameters

None

Return value

A string containing the HTML representation of the element.

Description

This method is not available on XML documents.

In an HTML document, we can use `.html()` to get the contents of any element. If our selector expression matches more than one element, only the first one's HTML content is returned. Consider the following code:

```
$('div.demo-container').html();
```

In order for the content of the following `<div>` to be retrieved, it would have to be the first one in the document.

```
<div class="demo-container">
  <div class="demo-box">Demonstration Box</div>
</div>
```

The result would look like this:

<div class="demo-box">Demonstration Box</div>

.html() (setter)

Set the HTML contents of each element in the set of matched elements.
```
.html(htmlString)
.html(function)
```

Parameters (first version)

- `htmlString`: A string of HTML to set as the content of each matched element

Parameters (second version)

• `function`: A function returning the HTML content to set

Return value

The jQuery object, for chaining purposes.

Description

The `.html()` method is not available in XML documents.

When we use `.html()` to set the content of elements, any content that was in those elements is completely replaced by the new content. Consider the following HTML code:

```
<div class="demo-container">
  <div class="demo-box">Demonstration Box</div>
</div>
```

We can set the HTML contents of `<div class="demo-container">` as follows:

```
$('div.demo-container')
  .html('<p>All new content. <em>You bet!</em></p>');
```

That line of code will replace everything inside `<div class="demo-container">`.

```
<div class="demo-container">
  <p>All new content. <em>You bet!</em></p>
</div>
```

As of jQuery 1.4, the `.html()` method allows us to set the HTML content by passing in a function.

```
$('div.demo-container').html(function() {
  var emph = '<em>' + $('p').length + ' paragraphs!</em>';
  return '<p>All new content for ' + emph + '</p>';
});
```

Given a document with six paragraphs, this example will set the HTML of `<div class="demo-container">` to `<p>All new content for <em>6 paragraphs!</em></p>`.

.text() (getter)

Get the combined text contents of each element in the set of matched elements, including their descendants.

```
.text()
```

Parameters

None

Return value

A string containing the combined text contents of the matched elements.

Description

Unlike the `.html()` method, `.text()` can be used in both XML and HTML documents. The result of the `.text()` method is a string containing the combined text of all matched elements. Consider the following HTML code:

```
<div class="demo-container">
  <div class="demo-box">Demonstration Box</div>
  <ul>
    <li>list item 1</li>
    <li>list <strong>item</strong> 2</li>
  </ul>
</div>
```

The code `$('div.demo-container').text()` would produce the following result:

Demonstration Box list item 1 list item 2

.text() (setter)

Set the content of each element in the set of matched elements to the specified text.

```
.text(textString)
.text(function)
```

Parameters (first version)

- `textString`: A string of text to set as the content of each matched element

Parameters (second version)

- `function`: A function returning the text to set as the content

Return value

The jQuery object, for chaining purposes.

Description

Unlike the `.html()` method, `.text()` can be used in both XML and HTML documents.

We need to be aware that this method escapes the string provided as necessary so that it will render correctly in HTML. To do so, it calls the DOM method `.createTextNode()`, which replaces special characters with their HTML entity equivalents (such as `&lt;` for `<`). Consider the following HTML code:

```
<div class="demo-container">
  <div class="demo-box">Demonstration Box</div>
  <ul>
    <li>list item 1</li>
    <li>list <strong>item</strong> 2</li>
  </ul>
</div>
```

The code `$('div.demo-container').text('<p>This is a test.</p>');` will produce the following DOM output:

```
<div class="demo-container">
  &lt;p&gt;This is a test.&lt;/p&gt;
</div>
```

It will appear on a rendered page as though the tags were exposed as follows:

<p>This is a test</p>

As of jQuery 1.4, the `.text()` method allows us to set the text content by passing in a function.

```
$('ul li').text(function() {
  return 'item number ' + ($(this).index() + 1);
});
```

Given an unordered list with three `<li>` elements, this example will produce the following DOM output:

```
<ul>
  <li>item number 1</li>
  <li>item number 2</li>
  <li>item number 3</li>
</ul>
```

.val() (getter)

Get the current value of the first element in the set of matched elements.

```
.val()
```

Parameters

None

Return value

A string containing the value of the element, or an array of strings if the element can have multiple values.

Description

The `.val()` method is primarily used to get the values of form elements. In the case of `<select multiple="multiple">` elements, the `.val()` method returns an array containing each selected option.

.val() (setter)

Set the value of each element in the set of matched elements.

```
.val(value)
.val(function)
```

Parameters (first version)

- `value`: A string of text or an array of strings to set as the value property of each matched element

Parameters (second version)

- `function`: A function returning the value to set

Return value

The jQuery object, for chaining purposes.

Description

This method is typically used to set the values of form fields. For `<select multiple="multiple">` elements, multiple `<option>` can be selected by passing in an array.

The `.val()` method allows us to set the value by passing in a function.

```
$('input:text.items').val(function() {
  return this.value + ' ' + this.className;
});
```

This example appends the string "items" to the text inputs' values.

.replaceWith()

Replace each element in the set of matched elements with the provided new content.

```
.replaceWith(newContent)
```

Parameters

- `newContent`: The content to insert. This might be an HTML string, a DOM element, or a jQuery object.

Return value

The jQuery object, for chaining purposes. See the following section for details.

Description

The `.replaceWith()` method allows us to remove content from the DOM and insert new content in its place with a single call. Consider this DOM structure:

```
<div class="container">
  <div class="inner first">Hello</div>
  <div class="inner second">And</div>
  <div class="inner third">Goodbye</div>
</div>
```

We can replace the second inner `<div>` with specified HTML.

```
$('.second').replaceWith('<h2>New heading</h2>');
```

This results in the following structure:

```
<div class="container">
  <div class="inner first">Hello</div>
  <h2>New heading</h2>
  <div class="inner third">Goodbye</div>
</div>
```

We could equally target all inner `<div>` elements at once.

```
$('.inner').replaceWith('<h2>New heading</h2>');
```

This causes all of them to be replaced.

```
<div class="container">
  <h2>New heading</h2>
  <h2>New heading</h2>
  <h2>New heading</h2>
</div>
```

Alternatively, we could select an element to use as the replacement.

```
$('.third').replaceWith($('.first'));
```

This results in the following DOM structure:

```
<div class="container">
  <div class="inner second">And</div>
  <div class="inner first">Hello</div>
</div>
```

From this example, we can see that the selected element replaces the target by being moved from its old location, and not by being cloned.

The `.replaceWith()` method, like most jQuery methods, returns the jQuery object so that other methods can be chained onto it. However, it must be noted that the *original* jQuery object is returned. This object refers to the element that has been removed from the DOM, not the new element that has replaced it.

.replaceAll()

> Replace each target element with the set of matched elements.
>
>   .replaceAll(target)

Parameters

- `target`: A selector expression indicating which element(s) to replace

Return value

The jQuery object, for chaining purposes.

Description

The .replaceAll() method is corollary to .replaceWith(), but with the source and target reversed. Consider the following DOM structure:

```
<div class="container">
  <div class="inner first">Hello</div>
  <div class="inner second">And</div>
  <div class="inner third">Goodbye</div>
</div>
```

We can create an element, and then replace other elements with it.

```
$('<h2>New heading</h2>').replaceAll('.inner');
```

This causes all of them to be replaced.

```
<div class="container">
  <h2>New heading</h2>
  <h2>New heading</h2>
  <h2>New heading</h2>
</div>
```

Alternatively, we could select an element to use as the replacement:

```
$('.first').replaceAll('.third');
```

This results in the following DOM structure:

```
<div class="container">
  <div class="inner second">And</div>
  <div class="inner first">Hello</div>
</div>
```

From this example, we can see that the selected element replaces the target by being moved from its old location, and not by being cloned.

DOM insertion, inside

These methods allow us to insert new content inside an existing element.

.prepend()

Insert content specified by the parameter at the beginning of each element in the set of matched elements.

```
.prepend(content)
.prepend(function)
```

Parameters (first version)

- content: An element, an HTML string, or a jQuery object to insert at the beginning of each element in the set of matched elements

Parameters (second version)

- function: A function that returns an HTML string to insert at the beginning of each element in the set of matched elements

Return value

The jQuery object, for chaining purposes.

Description

The .prepend() and .prependTo() methods perform the same task. The major difference is in the syntax, specifically in the placement of the content and target. With .prepend(), the selector expression preceding the method is the container into which the content is inserted. With .prependTo(), on the other hand, the content precedes the method either as a selector expression or as markup created on the fly. It is then inserted into the target container.

Consider the following HTML code:

```
<h2>Greetings</h2>
<div class="container">
  <div class="inner">Hello</div>
  <div class="inner">Goodbye</div>
</div>
```

We can create content and insert it into several elements at once.

```
$('.inner').prepend('<p>Test</p>');
```

Each <div class="inner"> element gets the following new content:

```
<h2>Greetings</h2>
<div class="container">
  <div class="inner">
    <p>Test</p>
    Hello
  </div>
  <div class="inner">
    <p>Test</p>
    Goodbye
  </div>
</div>
```

We can also select an element on the page and insert it into another:

```
$('.container').prepend($('h2'));
```

If an element selected this way is inserted elsewhere, it will be moved into the target (not cloned).

```
<div class="container">
  <h2>Greetings</h2>
  <div class="inner">Hello</div>
  <div class="inner">Goodbye</div>
</div>
```

However, if there are more than one target elements, cloned copies of the inserted elements will be created for each target after the first.

.prependTo()

> Insert every element in the set of matched elements at the beginning of the target.
>
> ```
> .prependTo(target)
> ```

Parameters

- `target`: A selector, element, HTML string, or jQuery object; the matched set of elements will be inserted at the beginning of the element(s) specified by this parameter

Return value

The jQuery object, for chaining purposes.

Description

The `.prepend()` and `.prependTo()` methods perform the same task. The major difference is in the syntax, specifically in the placement of the content and target. With `.prepend()`, the selector expression preceding the method is the container into which the content is inserted. With `.prependTo()`, on the other hand, the content precedes the method either as a selector expression or as markup created on the fly, and is inserted into the target container.

Consider the following HTML code:

```
<h2>Greetings</h2>
<div class="container">
  <div class="inner">Hello</div>
  <div class="inner">Goodbye</div>
</div>
```

We can create content and insert it into several elements at once.

```
$('<p>Test</p>').prependTo('.inner');
```

Each inner `<div>` element gets the following new content:

```
<h2>Greetings</h2>
<div class="container">
  <div class="inner">
    <p>Test</p>
    Hello
  </div>
  <div class="inner">
    <p>Test</p>
    Goodbye
  </div>
</div>
```

We can also select an element on the page and insert it into another.

```
$('h2').prependTo($('.container'));
```

If an element selected this way is inserted elsewhere, it will be moved into the target (not cloned).

```
<div class="container">
  <h2>Greetings</h2>
  <div class="inner">Hello</div>
  <div class="inner">Goodbye</div>
</div>
```

However, if there are more than one target elements, cloned copies of the inserted elements will be created for each target after the first.

.append()

> Insert content specified by the parameter at the end of each element in the set of matched elements.
>
> ```
> .append(content)
> .append(function)
> ```

Parameters (first version)

- `content`: An element, an HTML string, or a jQuery object to insert at the end of each element in the set of matched elements

Parameters (second version)

- `function`: A function that returns an HTML string to insert at the end of each element in the set of matched elements

Return value

The jQuery object, for chaining purposes.

Description

The `.append()` and `.appendTo()` methods perform the same task. The major difference is in the syntax, specifically in the placement of the content and target. With `.append()`, the selector expression preceding the method is the container into which the content is inserted. With `.appendTo()`, on the other hand, the content precedes the method either as a selector expression or as markup created on the fly, and is inserted into the target container.

Consider the following HTML code:

```
<h2>Greetings</h2>
<div class="container">
  <div class="inner">Hello</div>
  <div class="inner">Goodbye</div>
</div>
```

We can create content and insert it into several elements at once.

```
$('.inner').append('<p>Test</p>');
```

Each inner `<div>` element gets the following new content:

```
<h2>Greetings</h2>
<div class="container">
  <div class="inner">
```

```
    Hello
    <p>Test</p>
  </div>
  <div class="inner">
    Goodbye
    <p>Test</p>
  </div>
</div>
```

We can also select an element on the page and insert it into another.

```
$('.container').append($('h2'));
```

If an element selected this way is inserted elsewhere, it will be moved into the target (not cloned).

```
<div class="container">
  <div class="inner">Hello</div>
  <div class="inner">Goodbye</div>
  <h2>Greetings</h2>
</div>
```

However, if there is more than one target element, cloned copies of the inserted elements will be created for each target after the first.

.appendTo()

Insert every element in the set of matched elements at the end of the target.

```
.appendTo(target)
```

Parameters

- `target`: A selector, element, HTML string, or jQuery object; the matched set of elements will be inserted at the end of the element(s) specified by this parameter

Return value

The jQuery object, for chaining purposes.

Description

The .append() and .appendTo() methods perform the same task. The major difference is in the syntax, specifically in the placement of the content and target. With .append(), the selector expression preceding the method is the container into which the content is inserted. With .appendTo(), on the other hand, the content precedes the method either as a selector expression or as markup created on the fly, and is inserted into the target container.

Consider the following HTML code:

```
<h2>Greetings</h2>
<div class="container">
  <div class="inner">Hello</div>
  <div class="inner">Goodbye</div>
</div>
```

We can create content and insert it into several elements at once.

```
$('<p>Test</p>').appendTo('.inner');
```

Each inner `<div>` element gets the following new content:

```
<h2>Greetings</h2>
<div class="container">
  <div class="inner">
    Hello
    <p>Test</p>
  </div>
  <div class="inner">
    Goodbye
    <p>Test</p>
  </div>
</div>
```

We can also select an element on the page and insert it into another.

```
$('h2').append($('.container'));
```

If an element selected this way is inserted elsewhere, it will be moved into the target (not cloned).

```
<div class="container">
  <div class="inner">Hello</div>
  <div class="inner">Goodbye</div>
  <h2>Greetings</h2>
</div>
```

However, if there are more than one target elements, cloned copies of the inserted elements will be created for each target after the first.

DOM insertion, outside

These methods allow us to insert new content outside an existing element.

.before()

Insert content specified by the parameter before each element in the set of matched elements.

```
.before(content)
.before(function)
```

Parameters (first version)

- content: An element, an HTML string, or a jQuery object to insert before each element in the set of matched elements

Parameters (second version)

- function: A function that returns an HTML string to insert before each element in the set of matched elements

Return value

The jQuery object, for chaining purposes.

Description

The .before() and .insertBefore() methods perform the same task. The major difference is in the syntax, specifically in the placement of the content and target. With .before(), the selector expression preceding the method is the container before which the content is inserted. With .insertBefore(), on the other hand, the content precedes the method either as a selector expression or as markup created on the fly, and is inserted before the target container.

Consider the following HTML code:

```
<div class="container">
  <h2>Greetings</h2>
  <div class="inner">Hello</div>
  <div class="inner">Goodbye</div>
</div>
```

We can create content and insert it before several elements at once.

```
$('.inner').before('<p>Test</p>');
```

Each inner `<div>` element gets the following new content:

```
<div class="container">
  <h2>Greetings</h2>
  <p>Test</p>
  <div class="inner">Hello</div>
  <p>Test</p>
  <div class="inner">Goodbye</div>
</div>
```

We can also select an element on the page and insert it before another.

```
$('.container').before($('h2'));
```

If an element selected this way is inserted elsewhere, it will be moved before the target (not cloned).

```
<h2>Greetings</h2>
<div class="container">
  <div class="inner">Hello</div>
  <div class="inner">Goodbye</div>
</div>
```

However, if there is more than one target element, cloned copies of the inserted elements will be created for each target after the first.

.insertBefore()

Insert every element in the set of matched elements before the target.

```
.insertBefore(target)
```

Parameters

- `target`: A selector, element, HTML string, or jQuery object; the matched set of elements will be inserted before the element(s) specified by this parameter.

Return value

The jQuery object, for chaining purposes.

Description

The `.before()` and `.insertBefore()` methods perform the same task. The major difference is in the syntax, specifically in the placement of the content and target. With `.before()`, the selector expression preceding the method is the container before which the content is inserted. With `.insertBefore()`, on the other hand, the content precedes the method either as a selector expression or as markup created on the fly, and is inserted before the target container.

Consider the following HTML code:

```html
<div class="container">
  <h2>Greetings</h2>
  <div class="inner">Hello</div>
  <div class="inner">Goodbye</div>
</div>
```

We can create content and insert it before several elements at once.

```javascript
$('<p>Test</p>').insertBefore('.inner');
```

Each inner `<div>` element gets the following new content:

```html
<div class="container">
  <h2>Greetings</h2>
  <p>Test</p>
  <div class="inner">Hello</div>
  <p>Test</p>
  <div class="inner">Goodbye</div>
</div>
```

We can also select an element on the page and insert it before another.

```javascript
$('h2').insertBefore($('.container'));
```

If an element selected this way is inserted elsewhere, it will be moved before the target (not cloned).

```html
<h2>Greetings</h2>
<div class="container">
  <div class="inner">Hello</div>
  <div class="inner">Goodbye</div>
</div>
```

However if there are more than one target elements, cloned copies of the inserted elements will be created for each target after the first.

.after()

Insert content specified by the parameter after each element in the set of matched elements.

```
.after(content)
.after(function)
```

Parameters (first version)

- content: An element, HTML string, or jQuery object to insert after each element in the set of matched elements

Parameters (second version)

- function: A function that returns an HTML string to insert after each element in the set of matched elements

Return value

The jQuery object, for chaining purposes.

Description

The .after() and .insertAfter() methods perform the same task. The major difference is in the syntax, specifically in the placement of the content and target. With .after(), the selector expression preceding the method is the container after which the content is inserted. With .insertAfter(), on the other hand, the content precedes the method either as a selector expression or as markup created on the fly, and is inserted after the target container.

Consider the following HTML code:

```
<div class="container">
  <h2>Greetings</h2>
  <div class="inner">Hello</div>
  <div class="inner">Goodbye</div>
</div>
```

We can create content and insert it after several elements at once.

```
$('.inner').after('<p>Test</p>');
```

Each inner `<div>` element gets the following new content:

```html
<div class="container">
  <h2>Greetings</h2>
  <div class="inner">Hello</div>
  <p>Test</p>
  <div class="inner">Goodbye</div>
  <p>Test</p>
</div>
```

We can also select an element on the page and insert it after another.

```javascript
$('.container').after($('h2'));
```

If an element selected this way is inserted elsewhere, it will be moved after the target (not cloned).

```html
<div class="container">
  <div class="inner">Hello</div>
  <div class="inner">Goodbye</div>
</div>
<h2>Greetings</h2>
```

However, if there are more than one target elements, cloned copies of the inserted element will be created for each target after the first.

.insertAfter()

Insert every element in the set of matched elements after the target.

```
.insertAfter(target)
```

Parameters

- `target`: A selector, element, HTML string, or jQuery object; the matched set of elements will be inserted after the element(s) specified by this parameter

Return value

The jQuery object, **for chaining** purposes.

Description

The .after() and .insertAfter() methods perform the same task. The major difference is in the syntax, specifically in the placement of the content and target. With .after(), the selector expression preceding the method is the container after which the content is inserted. With .insertAfter(), on the other hand, the content precedes the method either as a selector expression or as markup created on the fly, and is inserted after the target container.

Consider the following HTML code:

```
<div class="container">
  <h2>Greetings</h2>
  <div class="inner">Hello</div>
  <div class="inner">Goodbye</div>
</div>
```

We can create content and insert it after several elements at once.

```
$('<p>Test</p>').insertAfter('.inner');
```

Each inner <div> element gets the following content:

```
<div class="container">
  <h2>Greetings</h2>
  <div class="inner">Hello</div>
  <p>Test</p>
  <div class="inner">Goodbye</div>
  <p>Test</p>
</div>
```

We can also select an element on the page and insert it after another.

```
$('h2').insertAfter($('.container'));
```

If an element selected this way is inserted elsewhere, it will be moved after the target (not cloned).

```
<div class="container">
  <div class="inner">Hello</div>
  <div class="inner">Goodbye</div>
</div>
<h2>Greetings</h2>
```

However, if there are more than one target elements, cloned copies of the inserted elements will be created for each target after the first.

DOM insertion, around

These methods allow us to insert new content surrounding existing content.

.wrap()

Wrap an HTML structure around each element in the set of matched elements.

```
.wrap(wrappingElement)
.wrap(wrappingFunction)
```

Parameters (first version)

- wrappingElement: An HTML snippet, selector expression, jQuery object, or DOM element specifying the structure to wrap around the matched elements

Parameters (second version)

- wrappingFunction: A callback function that generates a structure to wrap around the matched elements

Return value

The jQuery object, for chaining purposes.

Description

The .wrap() function can take any string or object that could be passed to the $() factory function to specify a DOM structure. This structure may be nested several levels deep, but should contain only one inmost element. The structure will be wrapped around each of the elements in the set of matched elements.

Consider the following HTML code:

```
<div class="container">
  <div class="inner">Hello</div>
  <div class="inner">Goodbye</div>
</div>
```

Using .wrap(), we can insert an HTML structure around the inner <div> elements as follows:

```
$('.inner').wrap('<div class="new" />');
```

The new `<div>` element is created on the fly and added to the DOM. The result is a new `<div>` wrapped around each matched element.

```
<div class="container">
  <div class="new">
    <div class="inner">Hello</div>
  </div>
  <div class="new">
    <div class="inner">Goodbye</div>
  </div>
</div>
```

The second version of this method allows us to specify a callback function instead. This callback function will be called once for every matched element. It should return a DOM element, a jQuery object, or an HTML snippet in which to wrap the corresponding element. For example:

```
$('.inner').wrap(function() {
  return '<div class="' + $(this).text() + '" />';
});
```

This will cause each `<div>` to have a class corresponding to the text it wraps.

```
<div class="container">
  <div class="Hello">
    <div class="inner">Hello</div>
  </div>
  <div class="Goodbye">
    <div class="inner">Goodbye</div>
  </div>
</div>
```

.wrapAll()

Wrap an HTML structure around all elements in the set of matched elements.
`.wrapAll(wrappingElement)`

Parameters

- `wrappingElement`: An HTML snippet, selector expression, jQuery object, or DOM element specifying the structure to wrap around the matched elements

Return value

The jQuery object, for chaining purposes.

Description

The `.wrapAll()` function can take any string or object that could be passed to the `$()` factory function to specify a DOM structure. This structure may be nested several levels deep, but should contain only one inmost element. The structure will be wrapped around all of the elements in the set of matched elements as a single group.

Consider the following HTML code:

```
<div class="container">
  <div class="inner">Hello</div>
  <div class="inner">Goodbye</div>
</div>
```

Using `.wrapAll()`, we can insert an HTML structure around the inner `<div>` elements as follows:

```
$('.inner').wrapAll('<div class="new" />');
```

The new `<div>` element is created on the fly and added to the DOM. The result is a new `<div>` wrapped around all matched elements.

```
<div class="container">
  <div class="new">
    <div class="inner">Hello</div>
    <div class="inner">Goodbye</div>
  </div>
</div>
```

.wrapInner()

> Wrap an HTML structure around the content of each element in the set of matched elements.
>
> ```
> .wrapInner(wrappingElement)
> .wrapInner(wrappingFunction)
> ```

Parameters (first version)

- `wrappingElement`: An HTML snippet, a selector expression, a jQuery object, or a DOM element specifying the structure to wrap around the content of the matched elements

Parameters (second version)

- `wrappingFunction`: A callback function that generates a structure to wrap around the content of the matched elements

Return value

The jQuery object, for chaining purposes.

Description

The `.wrapInner()` function can take any string or object that could be passed to the `$()` factory function to specify a DOM structure. This structure may be nested several levels deep, but should contain only one inmost element. The structure will be wrapped around the content of each of the elements in the set of matched elements.

Consider the following HTML code:

```
<div class="container">
  <div class="inner">Hello</div>
  <div class="inner">Goodbye</div>
</div>
```

Using `.wrapInner()`, we can insert an HTML structure around the content of the inner `<div>` elements as follows:

```
$('.inner').wrapInner('<div class="new" />');
```

The new `<div>` element is created on the fly and added to the DOM. The result is a new `<div>` wrapped around the content of each matched element.

```
<div class="container">
  <div class="inner">     <div class="new">Hello</div>
  </div>
  <div class="inner">
    <div class="new">Goodbye</div>
  </div>
</div>
```

The second version of this method allows us to specify a callback function instead. This callback function will be called once for every matched element; it should return a DOM element, jQuery object, or HTML snippet in which to wrap the content of the corresponding element. For example:

```
$('.inner').wrapInner(function() {
  return '<div class="' + this.nodeValue + '" />';
});
```

This will cause each new `<div>` to have a class corresponding to the text it wraps.

```
<div class="container">
  <div class="inner">
    <div class="Hello">Hello</div>
  </div>
  <div class="inner">
    <div class="Goodbye">Goodbye</div>
  </div>
</div>
```

DOM copying

This method allows us to make copies of elements.

.clone()

Create a copy of the set of matched elements.
```
.clone([withEvents])
```

Parameters

- `withEvents` (optional): A Boolean indicating whether event handlers should be copied along with the elements

Return value

A new jQuery object referencing the created elements.

Description

The `.clone()` method, when used in conjunction with one of the insertion methods, is a convenient way to duplicate elements on a page. Consider the following HTML code:

```
<div class="container">
  <div class="hello">Hello</div>
  <div class="goodbye">Goodbye</div>
</div>
```

As shown in the *Description* for `.append()`, normally when we insert an element somewhere in the DOM, it is moved from its old location. So, suppose this code is used:

```
$('.hello').appendTo('.goodbye');
```

The resulting DOM structure will be as follows:

```
<div class="container">
  <div class="goodbye">
    Goodbye
    <div class="hello">Hello</div>
  </div>
</div>
```

To prevent this and instead create a copy of the element, we could write the following:

```
$('.hello').clone()
.appendTo('.goodbye');
```

This will produce the following:

```
<div class="container">
  <div class="hello">Hello</div>
  <div class="goodbye">
    Goodbye
    <div class="hello">Hello</div>
  </div>
</div>
```

> Note that when using the .clone() method, we can modify the cloned elements or their contents before (re-)inserting them into the document.

Normally, any event handlers bound to the original element are *not* copied to the clone. The optional withEvents parameter allows us to change this behavior, and instead make copies of all the event handlers as well, bound to the new copy of the element. As of jQuery 1.4, all element data attached by the .data() method will be copied along with the event handlers.

DOM removal

These methods allow us to delete elements from the DOM.

.empty()

Remove all child nodes of the set of matched elements from the DOM.
.empty()

Parameters

None

Return value

The jQuery object, for chaining purposes.

Description

This method removes not only child (and other descendant) elements, but also any text within the set of matched elements. This is because according to the DOM specification, any string of text within an element is considered a child node of that element. Consider the following HTML code:

```
<div class="container">
  <div class="hello">Hello</div>
  <div class="goodbye">Goodbye</div>
</div>
```

We can target any element for removal.

```
$('.hello').empty();
```

This will result in a DOM structure with the "Hello" text deleted.

```
<div class="container">
  <div class="hello"></div>
  <div class="goodbye">Goodbye</div>
</div>
```

If we had any number of nested elements inside `<div class="hello">`, they would be removed, too. Other jQuery constructs such as data or event handlers are erased as well.

.remove()

Remove the set of matched elements from the DOM.
```
.remove([selector])
```

Parameters

- `selector` (optional): A selector expression that filters the set of matched elements to be removed

Return value

The jQuery object, for chaining purposes. Note that the removed elements are still referenced by this object, even though they are no longer in the DOM.

Description

Similar to `.empty()`, the `.remove()` method takes elements out of the DOM. We use `.remove()` when we want to remove the element itself, as well as everything inside it. In addition to the elements themselves, all bound events and jQuery data associated with the elements are removed.

Consider the following HTML code:

```
<div class="container">
  <div class="hello">Hello</div>
  <div class="goodbye">Goodbye</div>
</div>
```

We can target any element for removal.

```
$('.hello').remove();
```

This will result in a DOM structure with the `<div>` element deleted.

```
<div class="container">
  <div class="goodbye">Goodbye</div>
</div>
```

If we had any number of nested elements inside `<div class="hello">`, they would be removed, too. Other jQuery constructs such as data or event handlers are erased as well.

We can also include a selector as an optional parameter. For example, we could rewrite the previous DOM removal code as follows:

```
$('div').remove('.hello');
```

This would result in the same DOM structure.

```
<div class="container">
  <div class="goodbye">Goodbye</div>
</div>
```

.detach()

> Remove the set of matched elements from the DOM.
>
> ```
> .detach([selector])
> ```

Parameters

- `selector` (optional): A selector expression that filters the set of matched elements to be removed.

Return value

The jQuery object, for chaining purposes. Note that the removed elements are still referenced by this object, even though they are no longer in the DOM.

Description

The `.detach()` method is the same as `.remove()`, except that `.detach()` keeps all jQuery data associated with the removed elements. This method is useful when removed elements are to be reinserted into the DOM at a later time.

.unwrap()

> Remove the parents of the set of matched elements from the DOM, leaving the matched elements in their place.
>
> ```
> .unwrap()
> ```

Parameters

None

Return value

The jQuery object, for chaining purposes.

Description

The `.unwrap()` method removes the element's parent. This is effectively the inverse of the `.wrap()` method. The matched elements (and their siblings, if any) replace their parents within the DOM structure.

5

Event Methods

The jQuery library allows us to observe user and browser behavior, and react accordingly. In this chapter, we'll closely examine each of the available event methods in turn. These methods are used to register behaviors to take effect when the user interacts with the browser, and to further manipulate those registered behaviors.

 Some of the examples in this chapter use the $.print() function to print results to the page. This is a simple plug-in, which will be discussed in Chapter 10, *Plug-in API*.

Event handler attachment

The following methods are the building blocks of jQuery's event handling module.

.bind()

Attach a handler to an event for the elements.

    .bind(eventType[, eventData], handler)

Parameters

- eventType: A string containing one or more JavaScript event types such as click, submit, or custom event names
- eventData (optional): A map of data that will be passed to the event handler
- handler: A function to execute each time the event is triggered

Return value

The jQuery object, for chaining purposes.

Description

The .bind() method is the primary means of attaching behavior to a document. All JavaScript event types such as focus, mouseover, and resize are allowed for eventType.

The jQuery library provides shortcut methods for binding the standard event types such as .click() for .bind('click'). Details of each event type can be found in the *Description* of its shortcut method.

Any string is legal for eventType. If the string is not the name of a native JavaScript event, then the handler is bound to a **custom event**. These events are never called by the browser, but may be triggered manually from other JavaScript code using .trigger() or .triggerHandler().

If the eventType string contains a period (.) character, then the event is **namespaced**. The period character separates the event from its namespace. For example, in the call .bind('click.name', handler), the string click is the event type and the string name is the namespace. Namespacing allows us to unbind or trigger some events of a type without affecting others. See the *Description* of .unbind() for more information.

When an event reaches an element, all handlers bound to that event type for the element are fired. If there are multiple handlers registered, they will always execute in the order in which they were bound. After all handlers have executed, the event continues along the normal event propagation path.

 For an in-depth description of event propagation, see Chapter 3 of the book *Learning jQuery 1.3*.

A basic usage of .bind() is:

```
$('#foo').bind('click', function() {
  alert('User clicked on "foo."');
});
```

This code will cause the element with an ID of foo to respond to the click event. When a user clicks inside this element thereafter, the alert will be shown.

Event handlers

The `handler` parameter takes a callback function, as previously shown. Within the handler, the keyword `this` refers to the DOM element to which the handler is bound. To make use of the element in jQuery, it can be passed to the normal `$()` function. For example:

```
$('#foo').bind('click', function() {
  alert($(this).text());
});
```

After this code is executed, whenever the user clicks inside the element with an ID of `foo`, its text contents will be shown as an alert.

The event object

The `handler` callback function can also take parameters. When the function is called, the JavaScript event object will be passed to the first parameter.

The event object is often unnecessary and the parameter is omitted, as sufficient context is usually available when the handler is bound to know exactly what needs to be done when the handler is triggered. However, at times it becomes necessary to gather more information about the user's environment at the time the event was initiated. JavaScript provides information such as `.shiftKey` (whether the *Shift* key was held down at the time), `.offsetX` (the *x* coordinate of the mouse cursor within the element), and `.type` (to determine which kind of event this is).

Some of the event object's attributes and methods are not available on every platform. If the event is handled by a jQuery event handler, however, the library standardizes certain attributes so that they can be safely used on any browser. The following attributes are standardized in particular:

- `.target`: This attribute represents the DOM element that initiated the event. It is often useful to compare `event.target` to `this` in order to determine if the event is being handled due to event bubbling.

- `.relatedTarget`: This attribute represents the other DOM element involved in the event, if any. For `mouseout`, it indicates the element being entered, and for `mousein`, it indicates the element being exited.

- `.which`: For the key or button events, this attribute indicates the specific key or button that was pressed.

- `.pageX`: This attribute contains the *x* coordinate of the mouse cursor relative to the left edge of the page.

- `.pageY`: This attribute contains the *y* coordinate of the mouse cursor relative to the top edge of the page.

- `.result`: This attribute contains the last value returned by an event handler that was triggered by this event, unless the value was `undefined`.

- `.timeStamp`: This attribute returns the number of milliseconds since January 1, 1970 when the event is triggered. It can be useful for profiling the performance of certain jQuery functions.

- `.preventDefault()`: If this method is called, the default action of the event will not be triggered. For example, clicked anchors will not take the browser to a new URL. We can use `.isDefaultPrevented()` to determine if this method has been called by an event handler that was triggered by this event.

- `.stopPropagation()`: This method prevents the event from bubbling up the DOM tree looking for more event handlers to trigger. We can use `.isPropagationStopped()` to determine if this method has been called by an event handler that was triggered by this event.

Returning `false` from a handler is equivalent to calling both `.preventDefault()` and `.stopPropagation()` on the event object.

Using the event object in a handler looks like this:

```
$(document).ready(function() {
  $('#foo').bind('click', function(event) {
    alert('The mouse cursor is at ('
      + event.pageX + ', ' + event.pageY + ')');
  });
});
```

Note the parameter added to the anonymous function. This code will cause a click on the element with ID `foo` to report the page coordinates of the mouse cursor at the time of the click.

Passing event data

The optional `eventData` parameter is not commonly used. When provided, this argument allows us to pass additional information to the handler. One handy use of this parameter is to work around issues caused by **closures**. For example, suppose we have two event handlers that both refer to the same external variable.

```
var message = 'Spoon!';
$('#foo').bind('click', function() {
  alert(message);
});
message = 'Not in the face!';
$('#bar').bind('click', function() {
  alert(message);
});
```

As the handlers are closures having `message` in their environment, both will display the message **Not in the face!** when triggered. The variable's value has changed. To sidestep this, we can pass the message in using `eventData`.

```
var message = 'Spoon!';
$('#foo').bind('click', {msg: message}, function(event) {
  alert(event.data.msg);
});
message = 'Not in the face!';
$('#bar').bind('click', {msg: message}, function(event) {
  alert(event.data.msg);
});
```

This time the variable is not referred to directly within the handlers. Instead, the variable is passed in *by value* through `eventData`, which fixes the value at the time the event is bound. The first handler will now display **Spoon!**, while the second will alert **Not in the face!**.

 Note that objects are passed to functions *by reference*, which further complicates this scenario. An in-depth description of closures can be found in Appendix C of the book *Learning jQuery 1.3*.

If `eventData` is present, it is the second argument to the `.bind()` method. If no additional data needs to be sent to the handler, then the callback is passed as the second and final argument.

 See the `.trigger()` method reference for a way to pass data to a handler at the time the event happens rather than when the handler is bound.

.unbind()

Remove a previously-attached event handler from the elements.

```
.unbind([eventType[, handler]])
.unbind(event)
```

Parameters (first version)

- `eventType`: A string containing a JavaScript event type such as `click` or `submit`
- `handler`: The function that is to be no longer executed

Parameters (second version)

- `event`: A JavaScript event object as passed to an event handler

Return value

The jQuery object, for chaining purposes.

Description

Any handler that has been attached with `.bind()` can be removed with `.unbind()`. In the simplest case with no arguments, `.unbind()` removes all handlers attached to the elements.

```
$('#foo').unbind();
```

This version removes the handlers regardless of type. To be more precise, we can pass an event type.

```
$('#foo').unbind('click');
```

By specifying the `click` event type, only handlers for that event type will be unbound. However, this approach can still have negative ramifications if other scripts might be attaching behaviors to the same element. Robust and extensible applications typically demand the two-argument version for this reason.

```
var handler = function() {
  alert('The quick brown fox jumps over the lazy dog.');
};
$('#foo').bind('click', handler);
$('#foo').unbind('click', handler);
```

By naming the handler, we can be assured that no other functions are caught in the crossfire. Note that the following will *not* work:

```
$('#foo').bind('click', function() {
  alert('The quick brown fox jumps over the lazy dog.');
});

$('#foo').unbind('click', function() {
  alert('The quick brown fox jumps over the lazy dog.');
});
```

Even though the two functions are identical in content, they are created separately and so JavaScript is free to keep them as distinct function objects. To unbind a particular handler, we need a reference to that function and not a different one that happens to do the same thing.

Using namespaces

Instead of maintaining references to handlers in order to unbind them, we can **namespace** the events and use this capability to narrow the scope of our unbinding actions. As shown in the *Description* for the .bind() method, namespaces are defined by using a period (.) character when binding a handler.

```
$('#foo').bind('click.myEvents', handler);
```

When a handler is bound in this fashion, we can still unbind it the normal way.

```
$('#foo').unbind('click');
```

However, if we want to avoid affecting other handlers, we can be more specific.

```
$('#foo').unbind('click.myEvents');
```

If multiple namespaced handlers are bound, we can unbind them at once.

```
$('#foo').unbind('click.myEvents.yourEvents');
```

This syntax is similar to that used for CSS class selectors; they are not hierarchical. This method call is thus the same as the following:

```
$('#foo').unbind('click.yourEvents.myEvents');
```

We can also unbind all of the handlers in a namespace, regardless of event type.

```
$('#foo').unbind('.myEvents');
```

It is particularly useful to attach namespaces to event bindings when we are developing plug-ins or otherwise writing code that may interact with other event-handling code in the future.

Using the event object

The second form of the .unbind() method is used when we wish to unbind a handler from within itself. For example, suppose we wish to trigger an event handler only three times:

```
var timesClicked = 0;
$('#foo').bind('click', function(event) {
  alert('The quick brown fox jumps over the lazy dog.');
  timesClicked++;
  if (timesClicked >= 3) {
    $(this).unbind(event);
  }
});
```

The handler, in this case, must take a parameter so that we can capture the event object and use it to unbind the handler after the third click. The event object contains the context necessary for `.unbind()` to know which handler to remove.

This example is also an illustration of a **closure**. As the handler refers to the `timesClicked` variable, which is defined outside the function, incrementing the variable has an effect even between invocations of the handler.

.one()

Attach a handler to an event for the elements. The handler is executed at most once.

```
.one(eventType[, eventData], handler)
```

Parameters

* `eventType`: A string containing a JavaScript event type such as `click` or `submit`
* `eventData` (optional): A map of data that will be passed to the event handler
* `handler`: A function to execute at the time the event is triggered

Return value

The jQuery object, for chaining purposes.

Description

This method is identical to `.bind()`, except that the handler is unbound after its first invocation. For example:

```
$('#foo').one('click', function() {
  alert('This will be displayed only once.');
});
```

After the code is executed, a click on the element with ID `foo` will display the alert. Subsequent clicks will do nothing.

This code is equivalent to the following:

```
$('#foo').bind('click', function(event) {
  alert('This will be displayed only once.');
  $(this).unbind(event);
});
```

In other words, explicitly calling the `.unbind()` from within a regularly bound handler has exactly the same effect.

.trigger()

> Execute all handlers and behaviors attached to the matched elements for the given event type.
>
> ```
> .trigger(eventType[, extraParameters])
> ```

Parameters

- `eventType`: A string containing a JavaScript event type such as `click` or `submit`

- `extraParameters`: An array of additional parameters to pass along to the event handler

Return value

The jQuery object, for chaining purposes.

Description

Any event handlers attached with `.bind()` or one of its shortcut methods are triggered when the corresponding event occurs. However, they can be fired manually with the `.trigger()` method. A call to `.trigger()` executes the handlers in the same order they would be if the event were triggered naturally by the user.

```
$('#foo').bind('click', function() {
  alert($(this).text());
});
$('#foo').trigger('click');
```

While `.trigger()` simulates an event activation, complete with a synthesized event object, it does not perfectly replicate a naturally occurring event.

When we define a custom event type using the `.bind()` method, the second argument to `.trigger()` can become useful. For example, suppose we have bound a handler for the `custom` event to our element instead of the built-in `click` event as done previously:

```
$('#foo').bind('custom', function(event, param1, param2) {
  alert(param1 + "\n" + param2);
});
$('#foo').trigger('custom', ['Custom', 'Event']);
```

The event object is always passed as the first parameter to an event handler. However, if additional parameters are specified during a `.trigger()` call as they are here, these parameters will be passed along to the handler as well.

Note the difference between the extra parameters we're passing here and the eventData parameter to the .bind() method. Both are mechanisms for passing information to an event handler. However, the extraParameters argument to .trigger() allows information to be determined at the time the event is triggered, while the eventData argument to .bind() requires the information to be already computed at the time the handler is bound.

.triggerHandler()

> Execute all handlers attached to an element for an event.
>
> .triggerHandler(eventType[, extraParameters])

Parameters

- eventType: A string containing a JavaScript event type such as click or submit

- extraParameters: An array of additional parameters to pass along to the event handler

Return value

The return value of the triggered handler, or undefined if no handlers are triggered.

Description

The .triggerHandler() method behaves similarly to .trigger(), with the following exceptions:

- The .triggerHandler() method does not cause the default behavior of an event to occur (such as a form submission)

- While .trigger() will operate on all elements matched by the jQuery object, .triggerHandler() only affects the first matched element

- Events created with .triggerHandler() do not bubble up the DOM hierarchy; if they are not handled by the target element directly, they do nothing

- Instead of returning the jQuery object (to allow chaining), .triggerHandler() returns whatever value was returned by the last handler it caused to be executed

For more information on this method, see the *Description* for .trigger().

.live()

> Attach a handler to the event for all elements that match the current selector, now or in the future.
>
> ```
> .live(eventType, handler)
> ```

Parameters

- `eventType`: A string containing a JavaScript event type such as `click` or `keydown`
- `handler`: A function to execute each time the event is triggered

Return value

The jQuery object, for chaining purposes.

Description

This method is a variation on the basic `.bind()` method for attaching event handlers to elements. When `.bind()` is called, the elements that the jQuery object refers to get the handler attached; however, the elements that get introduced later do not, so they would require another `.bind()` call. For instance, consider the following HTML code:

```
<body>
  <div class="clickme">
    Click here
  </div>
</body>
```

We can bind a simple click handler to this element.

```
$('.clickme').bind('click', function() {
  $.print('Bound handler called.');
});
```

When the element is clicked, the message gets printed. However, suppose that another element is added after this.

```
$('body').append('<div class="clickme">Another target</div>');
```

This new element also matches the selector `.clickme`, but since it was added after the call to `.bind()`, clicks on it will do nothing.

The `.live()` method provides an alternative to this behavior. Suppose we bind a click handler to the target element using this method.

```
$('.clickme').live('click', function() {
  $.print('Live handler called.');
});
```

And then we add a new element to this.

```
$('body').append('<div class="clickme">Another target</div>');
```

Then clicks on the new element will also trigger the handler.

Event delegation

The `.live()` method is able to affect elements that have not yet been added to the DOM through the use of **event delegation**—a handler bound to an ancestor element is responsible for events that are triggered on its descendants. The handler passed to `.live()` is never bound to an element; instead, `.live()` binds a special handler to the root of the DOM tree. In our example, when the new element is clicked, the following steps occur:

1. A click event is generated and passed to the `<div>` for handling.
2. No handler is directly bound to the `<div>`, so the event bubbles up the DOM tree.
3. The event bubbles up until it reaches the root of the tree, which is where `.live()` always binds its special handlers.
4. The special `click` handler bound by `.live()` executes.
5. This handler tests the `target` of the event object to see whether it should continue. This test is performed by checking if `$(event.target).closest('.clickme')` is able to locate a matching element.
6. If a matching element is found, the original handler is called on it.

As the test in step 5 is not performed until the event occurs, elements can be added at any time and still respond to events.

Caveats

The .live() technique is useful. However, due to its special approach, it cannot be simply substituted for .bind() in all cases. Specific differences include the following:

- Not all event types are supported. Only custom events and the following JavaScript events may be bound with .live():
    ◦ click
    ◦ dblclick
    ◦ keydown
    ◦ keypress
    ◦ keyup
    ◦ mousedown
    ◦ mousemove
    ◦ mouseout
    ◦ mouseover
    ◦ mouseup

- DOM traversal methods are not fully supported for finding elements to send to .live(). Rather, the .live() method should always be called directly after a selector, as in the previous example.

- To stop further handlers from executing after one bound using .live(), the handler must return false. Calling .stopPropagation() will not accomplish this.

See the *Description* for .bind() for more information on event binding.

.die()

> Remove an event handler previously attached using .live() from the elements.
>
>   .die(eventType[, handler])

Parameters

- eventType: A string containing a JavaScript event type such as click or keydown

- handler (optional): The function that is to be no longer executed

Return value

The jQuery object, for chaining purposes.

Description

Any handler that has been attached with .live() can be removed with .die().
This method is analogous to .unbind(), which is used to remove handlers attached
with .bind().

See the *Description* of .live() and .unbind() for further details.

Document loading

These events deal with the loading of a page into the browser.

.ready()

Specify a function to execute when the DOM is fully loaded.

```
$(document).ready(handler)
$().ready(handler)
$(handler)
```

Parameters

*   handler: A function to execute after the DOM is ready

Return value

The jQuery object, for chaining purposes.

Description

While JavaScript provides the load event for executing code when a page is
rendered, this event does not get triggered until all assets, such as images, have
been completely received. In most cases, the script can be run as soon as the DOM
hierarchy has been fully constructed. The handler passed to .ready() is guaranteed
to be executed after the DOM is ready, so this is usually the best place to attach all
other event handlers and run other jQuery code. When using scripts that rely on
the value of CSS style properties, it's important to reference external stylesheets or
embed style elements before referencing the scripts.

In cases where code relies on loaded assets (for example, if the dimensions of an image are required), the code should be placed in a handler for the `load` event instead.

 The `.ready()` method is generally incompatible with the `<body onload="">` attribute. If `load` must be used, either do not use `.ready()` or use jQuery's `.load()` method to attach `load` event handlers to the window or to more specific items such as images.

All three syntaxes provided are equivalent. The `.ready()` method can only be called on a jQuery object matching the current document. So, the selector can be omitted.

The `.ready()` method is typically used with an anonymous function:

```
$(document).ready(function() {
  $.print('Handler for .ready() called.');
});
```

With this code in place, the following message is printed when the page is loaded:

Handler for .ready() called.

If `.ready()` is called after the DOM has been initialized, the new handler passed in will be executed immediately.

Aliasing the jQuery namespace

When using another JavaScript library, we may wish to call `$.noConflict()` to avoid namespace difficulties. When this function is called, the `$` shortcut is no longer available, forcing us to write `jQuery` each time we would normally write `$`. However, the handler passed to the `.ready()` method can take an argument, which is passed the global `jQuery` object. This means we can rename the object within the context of our `.ready()` handler without affecting other code.

```
jQuery(document).ready(function($) {
  // Code using $ as usual goes here.
});
```

.load()

Bind an event handler to the `load` JavaScript event.

    `.load(handler)`

Parameters

- `handler`: A function to execute when the event is triggered

Return value

The jQuery object, for chaining purposes.

Description

This method is a shortcut for `.bind('load', handler)`.

The `load` event is sent to an element when it and all its sub-elements have been completely loaded. This event can be sent to any element associated with a URL such as images, scripts, frames, and the body of the document itself.

 It is possible that the load event will not be triggered if the image is loaded from the browser cache. To account for this possibility, we can test the value of the image's `.complete` property.

For example, consider a page with a simple image as follows:

```
<img src="book.png" alt="Book" id="book" />
```

The event handler can be bound to the image.

```
$('#book').load(function() {
  $.print('Handler for .load() called.');
});
```

Now as soon as the image has been loaded, the following message is displayed:

Handler for .load() called.

In general, it is not necessary to wait for all images to be fully loaded. If code can be executed earlier, it is usually best to place it in a handler sent to the `.ready()` method.

 The AJAX module also has a method named `.load()`; which one is fired depends on the set of arguments passed.

.unload()

> Bind an event handler to the unload JavaScript event.
>   .unload(handler)

Parameters

- handler: A function to execute when the event is triggered

Return value

The jQuery object, for chaining purposes.

Description

This method is a shortcut for .bind('unload', handler).

The unload event is sent to the window element when the user navigates away from the page. This could mean one of many things. The user could have clicked on a link to leave the page, or typed in a new URL in the address bar. The forward and back buttons will trigger the event. Closing the browser window will cause the event to be triggered. Even a page reload will first create an unload event.

> The exact handling of the unload event has varied from version to version of browsers. For example, some versions of Firefox trigger the event when a link is followed, but not when the window is closed. In practical usage, behavior should be tested on all supported browsers and contrasted with the proprietary beforeunload event.

Any unload event handler should be bound to the window object.

```
$(window).unload(function() {
  alert('Handler for .unload() called.');
});
```

After this code executes, the alert will be displayed whenever the browser leaves the current page.

It is not possible to cancel the unload event with .preventDefault(). This event is available so that scripts can perform cleanup when the user leaves the page.

.error()

Bind an event handler to the error JavaScript event.

```
.error(handler)
```

Parameters

- handler: A function to execute when the event is triggered

Return value

The jQuery object, for chaining purposes.

Description

This method is a shortcut for .bind('error', handler).

The error event is sent to elements such as images, which are referenced by a document and loaded by the browser. It is called if the element was not loaded correctly.

For example, consider a page with a simple image as follows:

```
<img src="missing.png" alt="Book" id="book" />
```

The event handler can be bound to the image.

```
$('#book').error(function() {
  $.print('Handler for .error() called.');
});
```

If the image cannot be loaded (for example, because it is not present at the supplied URL), the following message is displayed:

Handler for .error() called.

 This event may not be correctly fired when the page is served locally. As error relies on normal HTTP status codes, it will generally not be triggered if the URL uses the file: protocol.

Mouse events

These events are triggered by mouse movement and button presses.

.mousedown()

Bind an event handler to the mousedown JavaScript event, or trigger that event on an element.

```
.mousedown(handler)
.mousedown()
```

Parameters (first version)

- handler: A function to execute each time the event is triggered.

Return value

The jQuery object, for chaining purposes.

Description

This method is a shortcut for .bind('mousedown', handler) in the first variation and .trigger('mousedown') in the second.

The mousedown event is sent to an element when the mouse pointer is over the element and the mouse button is pressed. Any HTML element can receive this event.

For example, consider the following HTML code:

```
<div id="target">
  Click here
</div>
<div id="other">
  Trigger the handler
</div>
```

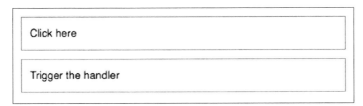

The event handler can be bound to any <div>.

```
$('#target').mousedown(function() {
  $.print('Handler for .mousedown() called.');
});
```

Now if we click on this element, the following message is displayed:

Handler for .mousedown() called.

We can also trigger the event when a different element is clicked.

```
$('#other').click(function() {
  $('#target').mousedown();
});
```

After this code executes, clicks on **Trigger the handler** will also display the same message.

The `mousedown` event is sent when any mouse button is clicked. To act only on specific buttons, we can use the event object's `.which` property. Not all browsers support this property (Internet Explorer uses `.button` instead), but jQuery normalizes the property so that it is safe to use in any browser. The value of `.which` will be 1 for the left button, 2 for the middle button, and 3 for the right button.

This event is primarily useful for ensuring that the primary button was used to begin a drag operation. If it is ignored, strange results can occur when the user attempts to use a context menu. While the middle and right buttons can be detected with these properties, this is not reliable. In Opera and Safari, for example, right mouse button clicks are not detectable by default.

If the user clicks on an element, drags away from it, and releases the button, this is still counted as a `mousedown` event. This sequence of actions is treated as a "canceling" of the button press in most user interfaces. So, it is usually better to use the `click` event unless we know that the `mousedown` event is preferable for a particular situation.

.mouseup()

Bind an event handler to the `mouseup` JavaScript event, or trigger that event on an element.

```
.mouseup(handler)
.mouseup()
```

Parameters (first version)
- `handler`: A function to execute each time the event is triggered

Return value
The jQuery object, for chaining purposes.

Description

This method is a shortcut for `.bind('mouseup', handler)` in the first variation, and `.trigger('mouseup')` in the second.

The `mouseup` event is sent to an element when the mouse pointer is over the element, and the mouse button is released. Any HTML element can receive this event.

For example, consider the following HTML code:

```
<div id="target">
  Click here
</div>
<div id="other">
  Trigger the handler
</div>
```

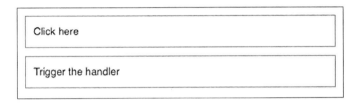

The event handler can be bound to any `<div>`.

```
$('#target').mouseup(function() {
  $.print('Handler for .mouseup() called.');
});
```

Now if we click on this element, the following message is displayed:

Handler for .mouseup() called.

We can also trigger the event when a different element is clicked.

```
$('#other').click(function() {
  $('#target').mouseup();
});
```

After this code executes, clicks on **Trigger the handler** will also display the same message.

If the user clicks outside an element, drags onto it, and releases the button, this is still counted as a `mouseup` event. This sequence of actions is not treated as a button press in most user interfaces, so it is usually better to use the `click` event unless we know that the `mouseup` event is preferable for a particular situation.

.click()

Bind an event handler to the `click` JavaScript event, or trigger that event on an element.

```
.click(handler)
.click()
```

Parameters (first version)

* `handler`: A function to execute each time the event is triggered.

Return value

The jQuery object, for chaining purposes.

Description

This method is a shortcut for `.bind('click', handler)` in the first variation, and `.trigger('click')` in the second.

The `click` event is sent to an element when the mouse pointer is over the element and the mouse button is pressed and released. Any HTML element can receive this event.

For example, consider the following HTML code:

```
<div id="target">
  Click here
</div>
<div id="other">
  Trigger the handler
</div>
```

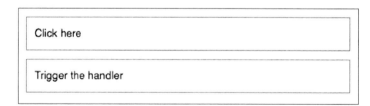

The event handler can be bound to any `<div>`.

```
$('#target').click(function() {
  $.print('Handler for .click() called.');
});
```

Now if we click on this element, the following message is displayed:

Handler for .click() called.

We can also trigger the event when a different element is clicked.

```
$('#other').click(function() {
  $('#target').click();
});
```

After this code executes, clicks on **Trigger the handler** will also display the same message.

The `click` event is only triggered after this exact series of events:

1. The mouse button is depressed while the pointer is inside the element.
2. The mouse button is released while the pointer is inside the element.

This is usually the desired sequence before taking an action. If this is not required, the `mousedown` or `mouseup` event may be more suitable.

.dblclick()

Bind an event handler to the `dblclick` JavaScript event, or trigger that event on an element.

```
.dblclick(handler)
.dblclick()
```

Parameters (first version)
- `handler`: A function to execute each time the event is triggered

Return value
The jQuery object, for chaining purposes.

Description
This method is a shortcut for `.bind('dblclick', handler)` in the first variation, and `.trigger('dblclick')` in the second.

The `dblclick` event is sent to an element when the element is double-clicked. Any HTML element can receive this event.

For example, consider the following HTML code:

```
<div id="target">
  Double-click here
</div>
<div id="other">
  Trigger the handler
</div>
```

The event handler can be bound to any `<div>`.

```
$('#target').dblclick(function() {
  $.print('Handler for .dblclick() called.');
});
```

Now if we double-click on this element, the following message is displayed:

Handler for .dblclick() called.

We can also trigger the event when a different element is clicked.

```
$('#other').click(function() {
  $('#target').dblclick();
});
```

After this code executes, (single) clicks on **Trigger the handler** will also display the same message.

The `dblclick` event is only triggered after this exact series of events:

1. The mouse button is depressed while the pointer is inside the element.
2. The mouse button is released while the pointer is inside the element.
3. The mouse button is depressed again while the pointer is inside the element within a time window that is system-dependent.
4. The mouse button is released while the pointer is inside the element.

It is inadvisable to ever bind handlers to both the `click` and `dblclick` events for the same element. The sequence of events triggered varies from browser to browser with some receiving two `click` events and others only one. If an interface that reacts differently to single and double clicks cannot be avoided, then the `dblclick` event should be simulated within the `click` handler. We can achieve this by saving a timestamp in the handler, and then comparing the current time to the saved timestamp on subsequent clicks. If the difference is small enough, we can treat the click as a double-click.

.toggle()

Bind two or more handlers to the matched elements, to be executed on alternate clicks.

```
.toggle(handlerEven, handlerOdd[,
    additionalHandlers...])
```

Parameters

- `handlerEven`: A function to execute every even time the element is clicked
- `handlerOdd`: A function to execute every odd time the element is clicked
- `additionalHandlers` (optional): Additional handlers to cycle through after clicks

Return value

The jQuery object, for chaining purposes.

Description

The `.toggle()` method binds a handler for the `click` event. So, the rules outlined for the triggering of `click` apply here as well.

For example, consider the following HTML code:

```
<div id="target">
  Click here
</div>
```

Event handlers can then be bound to the `<div>`.

```
$('#target').toggle(function() {
  $.print('First handler for .toggle() called.');
}, function() {
  $.print('Second handler for .toggle() called.');
});
```

As the element is clicked repeatedly, the messages alternate:

First handler for .toggle() called.

Second handler for .toggle() called.

First handler for .toggle() called.

Second handler for .toggle() called.

First handler for .toggle() called.

If more than two handlers are provided, `.toggle()` will cycle among all of them. For example, if there are three handlers, then the first handler will be called on the first click, the fourth click, the seventh click, and so on.

The `.toggle()` method is provided for convenience. It is relatively straightforward to implement the same behavior by hand, and this can be necessary if the assumptions built into `.toggle()` prove limiting. For example, `.toggle()` is not guaranteed to work correctly if applied twice to the same element. As `.toggle()` internally uses a `click` handler to do its work, we must unbind `click` to remove a behavior attached with `.toggle()` so that other `click` handlers can be caught in the crossfire. The implementation also calls `.preventDefault()` on the event. So links will not be followed and buttons will not be clicked if `.toggle()` has been called on the element.

.mouseover()

Bind an event handler to the mouseover JavaScript event, or trigger that event on an element.

```
.mouseover(handler)
.mouseover()
```

Parameters (first version)

- `handler`: A function to execute each time the event is triggered

Return value

The jQuery object, for chaining purposes.

Description

This method is a shortcut for `.bind('mouseover', handler)` in the first variation, and `.trigger('mouseover')` in the second.

The `mouseover` event is sent to an element when the mouse pointer enters the element. Any HTML element can receive this event.

For example, consider the following HTML code:

```
<div id="outer">
  Outer
  <div id="inner">
    Inner
  </div>
</div>
<div id="other">
  Trigger the handler
</div>
```

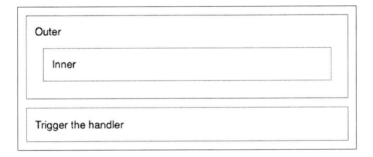

The event handler can be bound to any element.

```
$('#outer').mouseover(function() {
  $.print('Handler for .mouseover() called.');
});
```

Now when the mouse pointer moves over the **Outer** `<div>`, the following message is displayed:

Handler for .mouseover() called.

We can also trigger the event when another element is clicked.

```
$('#other').click(function() {
  $('#outer').mouseover();
});
```

After this code executes, clicks on **Trigger the handler** will also display the same message.

This event type can cause many headaches due to event bubbling. For instance, when the mouse pointer moves over the **Inner** element in this example, a mouseover event will be sent to that, and then it will trickle up to **Outer**. This can trigger our bound mouseover handler at inopportune times. See the *Description* for .mouseenter() for a useful alternative.

.mouseout()

Bind an event handler to the mouseout JavaScript event, or trigger that event on an element.

```
.mouseout(handler)
.mouseout()
```

Parameters (first version)
- handler: A function to execute each time the event is triggered

Return value
The jQuery object, for chaining purposes.

Description
This method is a shortcut for .bind('mouseout', handler) in the first variation, and .trigger('mouseout') in the second.

The mouseout event is sent to an element when the mouse pointer leaves the element. Any HTML element can receive this event.

For example, consider the following HTML code:

```
<div id="outer">
   Outer
   <div id="inner">
      Inner
   </div>
</div>
<div id="other">
   Trigger the handler
</div>
```

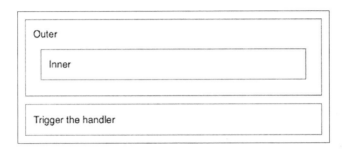

The event handler can be bound to any element.

```
$('#outer').mouseout(function() {
   $.print('Handler for .mouseout() called.');
});
```

Now when the mouse pointer moves out of the **Outer** <div>, the following message is displayed:

Handler for .mouseout() called.

We can also trigger the event when another element is clicked.

```
$('#other').click(function() {
   $('#outer').mouseout();
});
```

After this code executes, clicks on **Trigger the handler** will also display the same message.

This event type can cause many headaches due to event bubbling. For instance, when the mouse pointer moves out of the **Inner** element in this example, a mouseout event will be sent to that, and then it will trickle up to **Outer**. This can trigger our bound mouseout handler at inopportune times. See the *Description* for .mouseleave() for a useful alternative.

.mouseenter()

Bind an event handler to be fired when the mouse enters an element, or trigger that handler on an element.

```
.mouseenter(handler)
.mouseenter()
```

Parameters (first version)

- handler: A function to execute each time the event is triggered

Return value

The jQuery object, for chaining purposes.

Description

This method is a shortcut for .bind('mouseenter', handler) in the first variation, and .trigger('mouseenter') in the second.

The mouseenter JavaScript event is proprietary to Internet Explorer. Due to the event's general utility, jQuery simulates this event so that it can be used regardless of browser. This event is sent to an element when the mouse pointer enters the element. Any HTML element can receive this event.

For example, consider the following HTML code:

```
<div id="outer">
  Outer
  <div id="inner">
    Inner
  </div>
</div>
<div id="other">
  Trigger the handler
</div>
```

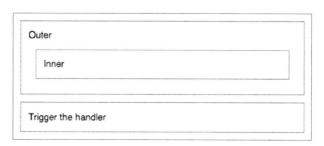

The event handler can be bound to any element.

```
$('#outer').mouseenter(function() {
  $.print('Handler for .mouseenter() called.');
});
```

Now when the mouse pointer moves over the **Outer** <div>, the following message is displayed:

Handler for .mouseenter() called.

We can also trigger the event when another element is clicked.

```
$('#other').click(function() {
  $('#outer').mouseenter();
});
```

After this code executes, clicks on **Trigger the handler** will also display the same message.

The mouseenter event differs from mouseover in the way it handles event bubbling. If mouseover was used in this example, then whenever the mouse pointer moved over the **Inner** element, the handler would be triggered. This is usually undesirable behavior. The mouseenter event, on the other hand, only triggers its handler when the mouse enters the element it is bound to (not a descendant). So in this example, the handler is triggered when the mouse enters the **Outer** element, but not the **Inner** element.

.mouseleave()

Bind an event handler to be fired when the mouse leaves an element, or trigger that handler on an element.

```
.mouseleave(handler)
.mouseleave()
```

Parameters (first version)

- handler: A function to execute each time the event is triggered

Return value

The jQuery object, for chaining purposes.

Description

This method is a shortcut for `.bind('mouseleave', handler)` in the first variation, and `.trigger('mouseleave')` in the second.

The `mouseleave` JavaScript event is proprietary to Internet Explorer. Because of the event's general utility, jQuery simulates this event so that it can be used regardless of the browser. This event is sent to an element when the mouse pointer leaves the element. Any HTML element can receive this event.

For example, consider the following HTML code:

```
<div id="outer">
  Outer
  <div id="inner">
    Inner
  </div>
</div>
<div id="other">
  Trigger the handler
</div>
```

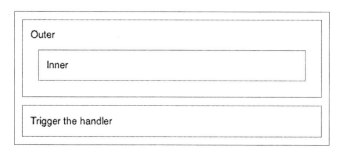

The event handler can be bound to any element.

```
$('#outer').mouseleave(function() {
  $.print('Handler for .mouseleave() called.');
});
```

Now when the mouse pointer moves out of the **Outer** `<div>`, the following message is displayed:

Handler for .mouseleave() called.

We can also trigger the event when another element is clicked.

```
$('#other').click(function() {
  $('#outer').mouseleave();
});
```

After this code executes, clicks on **Trigger the handler** will also display the same message.

The `mouseleave` event differs from `mouseout` in the way it handles event bubbling. If `mouseout` were used in this example, then when the mouse pointer moved out of the **Inner** element, the handler would be triggered. This is usually undesirable behavior. The `mouseleave` event, on the other hand, only triggers its handler when the mouse leaves the element it is bound to (not a descendant). So in this example, the handler is triggered when the mouse leaves the **Outer** element, but not the **Inner** element.

.hover()

Bind two handlers to the matched elements, to be executed when the mouse pointer enters and leaves the elements.

    .hover(handlerIn, handlerOut)

Parameters

- `handlerIn`: A function to execute when the mouse pointer enters the element
- `handlerOut`: A function to execute when the mouse pointer leaves the element

Return value

The jQuery object, for chaining purposes.

Description

The `.hover()` method binds handlers for both `mouseenter` and `mouseleave` events. We can use it to simply apply behavior to an element during the time the mouse is within the element.

Calling `$obj.hover(handlerIn, handlerOut)` is shorthand for the following:

```
$obj.mouseenter(handlerIn);
$obj.mouseleave(handlerOut);
```

See the *Description* for `.mouseenter()` and `.mouseleave()` for more details.

.mousemove()

Blind an event handler to the `mousemove` JavaScript event, or trigger that event on an element.

```
.mousemove(handler)
.mousemove()
```

Parameters (first version)

- `handler`: A function to execute each time the event is triggered

Return value

The jQuery object, for chaining purposes.

Description

This method is a shortcut for `.bind('mousemove', handler)` in the first variation, and `.trigger('mousemove')` in the second.

The `mousemove` event is sent to an element when the mouse pointer moves inside the element. Any HTML element can receive this event.

For example, consider the following HTML code:

```
<div id="target">
  Move here
</div>
<div id="other">
  Trigger the handler
</div>
```

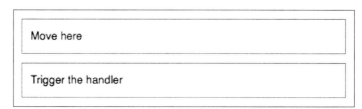

The event handler can be bound to the target:

```
$('#target').mousemove(function(event) {
  $.print('Handler for .mousemove() called at ('
    + event.pageX + ', ' + event.pageY + ')');
});
```

Now when the mouse pointer moves within the target button, the following messages are displayed:

Handler for .mousemove() called at (399, 48)

Handler for .mousemove() called at (398, 46)

Handler for .mousemove() called at (397, 44)

Handler for .mousemove() called at (396, 42)

We can also trigger the event when the second button is clicked.

```
$('#other').click(function() {
  $('#target').mousemove();
});
```

After this code executes, clicks on the **Trigger the handler** button will also display the following message:

Handler for .mousemove() called at (undefined, undefined)

When tracking mouse movement, we clearly usually need to know the actual position of the mouse pointer. The event object that is passed to the handler contains some information about the mouse coordinates. Properties such as .clientX, .offsetX, and .pageX are available, but support for them differs between browsers. Fortunately, jQuery normalizes the .pageX and .pageY attributes so that they can be used in all browsers. These attributes provide the X and Y coordinates of the mouse pointer relative to the top-left corner of the page, as illustrated in the preceding example output.

We need to remember that the mousemove event is triggered whenever the mouse pointer moves, even for a pixel. This means that hundreds of events can be generated over a very small amount of time. If the handler has to do any significant processing, or if multiple handlers for the event exist, this can be a serious performance drain on the browser. It is important, therefore, to optimize mousemove handlers as much as possible and to unbind them as soon as they are no longer needed.

A common pattern is to bind the mousemove handler from within a mousedown hander, and to unbind it from a corresponding mouseup handler. If you're implementing this sequence of events, remember that the mouseup event might be sent to a different HTML element than the mousemove event was. To account for this, the mouseup handler should typically be bound to an element high up in the DOM tree such as <body>.

Form events

These events refer to `<form>` elements and their contents.

.focus()

> Bind an event handler to the `focus` JavaScript event, or trigger that event on an element.
>
> `.focus(handler)`
> `.focus()`

Parameters (first version)

*   `handler`: A function to execute each time the event is triggered

Return value

The jQuery object, for chaining purposes.

Description

This method is a shortcut for `.bind('focus', handler)` in the first variation, and `.trigger('focus')` in the second.

The `focus` event is sent to an element when it gains focus. This event is implicitly applicable to a limited set of elements such as form elements (`<input>`, `<select>`, and others) and links (`<a href>`). In recent browser versions, the event can be extended to include all element types by explicitly setting the element's `tabindex` property. An element can gain focus via keyboard commands such as the *Tab* key, or by mouse clicks on the element.

Elements with focus are usually highlighted in some way by the browser, for example with a dotted line surrounding the element. The focus is used to determine which element is the first to receive keyboard-related events.

For example, consider the following HTML code:

```
<form>
  <input id="target" type="text" value="Field 1" />
  <input type="text" value="Field 2" />
</form>
<div id="other">
  Trigger the handler
</div>
```

The event handler can be bound to the first input field.

```
$('#target').focus(function() {
  $.print('Handler for .focus() called.');
});
```

Now if we click on the first field, or tab to it from another field, the following message is displayed:

Handler for .focus() called.

We can trigger the event when another element is clicked.

```
$('#other').click(function() {
  $('#target').focus();
});
```

After this code executes, clicks on **Trigger the handler** will also display the same message.

The focus event does not bubble in Internet Explorer. Therefore, scripts that rely on **event delegation** with the focus event will not work consistently across browsers.

 Triggering the focus on hidden elements causes an error in Internet Explorer. Take care to call .focus() without parameters only on elements that are visible.

.blur()

Bind an event handler to the blur JavaScript event, or trigger that event on an element.

```
.blur(handler)
.blur()
```

Parameters (first version)

- handler: A function to execute each time the event is triggered

Return value

The jQuery object, for chaining purposes.

Description

This method is a shortcut for .bind('blur', handler) in the first variation, and .trigger('blur') in the second.

The blur event is sent to an element when it loses focus. Originally, this event was only applicable to form elements such as <input>. In recent browsers, the domain of the event has been extended to include all element types. An element can lose focus via keyboard commands such as the *Tab* key, or by mouse clicks elsewhere on the page.

For example, consider the following HTML code:

```
<form>
  <input id="target" type="text" value="Field 1" />
  <input type="text" value="Field 2" />
</form>
<div id="other">
  Trigger the handler
</div>
```

The event handler can be bound to the first input field.

```
$('#target').blur(function() {
  $.print('Handler for .blur() called.');
});
```

Now if the first field has the focus and we click elsewhere, or tab away from it, the following message is displayed:

Handler for .blur() called.

We can trigger the event when another element is clicked.

```
$('#other').click(function() {
  $('#target').blur();
});
```

After this code executes, clicks on **Trigger the handler** will also display the same message.

The blur event does not bubble in Internet Explorer. Therefore, scripts that rely on **event delegation** with the blur event will not work consistently across browsers.

.change()

Bind an event handler to the change JavaScript event, or trigger that event on an element.

```
.change(handler)
.change()
```

Parameters (first version)

- `handler`: A function to execute each time the event is triggered

Return value

The jQuery object, for chaining purposes.

Description

This method is a shortcut for `.bind('change', handler)` in the first variation, and `.trigger('change')` in the second.

The change event is sent to an element when its value changes. This event is limited to `<input type="text">` fields, `<textarea>` boxes, and `<select>` elements. For select boxes, the event is fired immediately when the user makes a selection with the mouse. However, for the other element types, the event is deferred until the element loses focus.

For example, consider the following HTML code:

```
<form>
  <input class="target" type="text" value="Field 1" />
  <select class="target">
    <option value="option1" selected="selected">Option 1</option>
    <option value="option2">Option 2</option>
  </select>
</form>
<div id="other">
  Trigger the handler
</div>
```

The event handler can be bound to the text input and the select box.

```
$('.target').change(function() {
  $.print('Handler for .change() called.');
});
```

Now when the second option is selected from the dropdown, the following message is displayed:

Handler for .change() called.

It is also displayed if we change the text in the field and then click away. If the field loses focus without the contents having changed, though, the event is not triggered. We can trigger the event manually when another element is clicked.

```
$('#other').click(function() {
  $('.target').change();
});
```

After this code executes, clicks on **Trigger the handler** will also display the same message. The message will be displayed twice because the handler has been bound to the change event on both of the form elements.

The change event does not bubble in Internet Explorer. Therefore, scripts that rely on **event delegation** with the change event will not work consistently across browsers.

.select()

Bind an event handler to the select JavaScript event, or trigger that event on an element.

```
.select(handler)
.select()
```

Parameters (first version)

- handler: A function to execute each time the event is triggered

Return value

The jQuery object, for chaining purposes.

Description

This method is a shortcut for .bind('select', handler) in the first variation, and .trigger('select') in the second.

The select event is sent to an element when the user makes a text selection inside it. This event is limited to <input type="text"> fields and <textarea> boxes.

For example, consider the following HTML code:

```
<form>
  <input id="target" type="text" value="Hello ther<div id="other">
  Trigger the handler
</div>
```

The event handler can be bound to the text input.

```
$('#target').select(function() {
  $.print('Handler for .select() called.');
});
```

Now when any portion of the text is selected, the following message is displayed:

Handler for .select() called.

Merely setting the location of the insertion point will not trigger the event. We can trigger the event manually when another element is clicked.

```
$('#other').click(function() {
  $('#target').select();
});
```

After this code executes, clicks on the **Trigger the handler** button will also display the same message.

In addition, the default `select` action on the field will be fired, so the entire text field will be selected.

 The method for retrieving the current selected text differs from one browser to another. For a simple cross-platform solution, use the **fieldSelection** jQuery plug-in.

.submit()

Bind an event handler to the `submit` JavaScript event, or trigger that event on an element.

```
.submit(handler)
.submit()
```

Parameters (first version)

- `handler`: A function to execute each time the event is triggered

Return value

The jQuery object, for chaining purposes.

Description

This method is a shortcut for `.bind('submit', handler)` in the first variation, and `.trigger('submit')` in the second.

The `submit` event is sent to an element when the user is attempting to submit a form. It can only be attached to `<form>` elements. Forms can be submitted either by clicking an explicit `<input type="submit">` button, or by pressing *Enter* when a form element has focus.

> Depending on the browser, the *Enter* key may only cause a form submission if the form has exactly one text field, or only when there is a submit button present. The interface should not rely on a particular behavior for this key unless the issue is forced by observing the keypress event for presses of the *Enter* key.

For example, consider the following HTML code:

```
<form id="target" action="destination.html">
  <input type="text" value="Hello there" />
  <input type="submit" value="Go" />
</form>
<div id="other">
  Trigger the handler
</div>
```

The event handler can be bound to the form.

```
$('#target').submit(function() {
  $.print('Handler for .submit() called.');
  return false;
});
```

Now when the form is submitted, the following message is displayed:

Handler for .submit() called.

This happens prior to the actual submission. Therefore, we can cancel the submit action by calling `.preventDefault()` on the event object or by returning `false` from our handler. We can trigger the event manually when another element is clicked.

```
$('#other').click(function() {
  $('#target').submit();
});
```

After this code executes, clicks on **Trigger the handler** will also display the same message.

In addition, the default `submit` action on the form will be fired, so the form will be submitted.

The `submit` event does not bubble in Internet Explorer. Therefore, scripts that rely on **event delegation** with the `submit` event will not work consistently across browsers.

Keyboard events

These events are triggered by the keys on the keyboard.

.keydown()

Bind an event handler to the `keydown` JavaScript event, or trigger that event on an element.

```
.keydown(handler)
.keydown()
```

Parameters (first version)

- `handler`: A function to execute each time the event is triggered

Return value

The jQuery object, for chaining purposes.

Description

This method is a shortcut for `.bind('keydown', handler)` in the first variation, and `.trigger('keydown')` in the second.

The `keydown` event is sent to an element when the user first presses a key on the keyboard. It can be attached to any element, but the event is only sent to the element that has the focus. Focusable elements can vary between browsers, but form elements can always get focus so are reasonable candidates for this event type.

For example, consider the following HTML code:

```
<form>
  <input id="target" type="text" value="Hello there" />
</form>
<div id="other">
  Trigger the handler
</div>
```

The event handler can be bound to the input field.

```
$('#target').keydown(function() {
  $.print('Handler for .keydown() called.');
});
```

Now when the insertion point is inside the field and a key is pressed, the following message is displayed:

Handler for .keydown() called.

We can trigger the event manually when another element is clicked.

```
$('#other').click(function() {
  $('#target').keydown();
});
```

After this code executes, clicks on **Trigger the handler** will also display the same message.

If key presses anywhere need to be caught (for example, to implement global shortcut keys on a page), it is useful to attach this behavior to the document object. Because of event bubbling, all key presses will make their way up the DOM to the document object unless explicitly stopped.

To determine which key was pressed, we can examine the event object that is passed to the handler function. While browsers use differing attributes to store this information, jQuery normalizes the .which attribute so we can reliably use it to retrieve the key code. This code corresponds to a key on the keyboard, including codes for special keys such as the arrow keys. For catching actual text entry, .keypress() may be a better choice.

.keypress()

Bind an event handler to the keypress JavaScript event, or trigger that event on an element.

```
.keypress(handler)
.keypress()
```

Parameters (first version)

- `handler`: A function to execute each time the event is triggered

Return value

The jQuery object, for chaining purposes.

Description

This method is a shortcut for `.bind('keypress', handler)` in the first variation, and `.trigger('keypress')` in the second.

The `keypress` event is sent to an element when the browser registers keyboard input. This is similar to the `keydown` event, except in the case of key repeats. If the user presses and holds a key, a `keydown` event is triggered once, but separate `keypress` events are triggered for each inserted character. In addition, modifier keys (such as *Shift*) cause `keydown` events, but not `keypress` events.

A `keypress` event handler can be attached to any element, but the event is only sent to the element that has the focus. Focusable elements can vary between browsers, but form elements can always get focus and so are reasonable candidates for this event type.

For example, consider the following HTML code:

```
<form>
  <input id="target" type="text" value="Hello there" />
</form>
<div id="other">
  Trigger the handler
</div>
```

The event handler can be bound to the input field.

```
$('#target').keypress(function() {
  $.print('Handler for .keypress() called.');
});
```

Now when the insertion point is inside the field and a key is pressed, the following message is displayed:

Handler for .keypress() called.

The message repeats if the key is held down. We can trigger the event manually when another element is clicked.

```
$('#other').click(function() {
  $('#target').keypress();
});
```

After this code executes, clicks on **Trigger the handler** will also display the same message.

If key presses anywhere need to be caught (for example, to implement global shortcut keys on a page), it is useful to attach this behavior to the document object. Because of event bubbling, all key presses will make their way up the DOM to the document object unless explicitly stopped.

To determine which character was entered, we can examine the event object that is passed to the handler function. While browsers use differing attributes to store this information, jQuery normalizes the .which attribute so we can reliably use it to retrieve the character code.

Note that keydown and keyup provide a code indicating which key is pressed, while keypress indicates which character was entered. For example, a lowercase "a" will be reported as 65 by keydown and keyup, but as 97 by keypress. An uppercase "A" is reported as 97 by all events. Because of this distinction, when catching special keystrokes such as arrow keys, .keydown() or .keyup() is a better choice.

.keyup()

Bind an event handler to the keyup JavaScript event, or trigger that event on an element.

```
.keyup(handler)
.keyup()
```

Parameters (first version)

- handler: A function to execute each time the event is triggered

Return value

The jQuery object, for chaining purposes.

Description

This method is a shortcut for `.bind('keyup', handler)` in the first variation, and `.trigger('keyup')` in the second.

The `keyup` event is sent to an element when the user releases a key on the keyboard. It can be attached to any element, but the event is only sent to the element that has the focus. Focusable elements can vary between browsers, but form elements can always get focus so are reasonable candidates for this event type.

For example, consider the following HTML code:

```
<form>
  <input id="target" type="text" value="Hello there" />
</form>
<div id="other">
  Trigger the handler
</div>
```

The event handler can be bound to the input field.

```
$('#target').keyup(function() {
  $.print('Handler for .keyup() called.');
});
```

Now when the insertion point is inside the field and a key is pressed and released, the following message is displayed:

Handler for .keyup() called.

We can trigger the event manually when another element is clicked.

```
$('#other').click(function() {
  $('#target').keyup();
});
```

After this code executes, clicks on **Trigger the handler** will also display the same message.

If key presses anywhere need to be caught (for example, to implement global shortcut keys on a page), it is useful to attach this behavior to the `document` object. Because of event bubbling, all key presses will make their way up the DOM to the `document` object unless explicitly stopped.

To determine which key was pressed, we can examine the event object that is passed to the handler function. While browsers use differing attributes to store this information, jQuery normalizes the .which attribute so we can reliably use it to retrieve the key code. This code corresponds to a key on the keyboard, including codes for special keys such as the arrow keys. For catching actual text entry, .keypress() may be a better choice.

Browser events

These are events related to the entire browser window.

.resize()

Bind an event handler to the resize JavaScript event, or trigger that event on an element.

```
.resize(handler)
.resize()
```

Parameters (first version)

- handler: A function to execute each time the event is triggered

Return value

The jQuery object, for chaining purposes.

Description

This method is a shortcut for .bind('resize', handler) in the first variation, and .trigger('resize') in the second.

The resize event is sent to the window element when the size of the browser window changes.

```
$(window).resize(function() {
  $.print('Handler for .resize() called.');
});
```

Now whenever the browser window's size is changed, the following message is displayed:

Handler for .resize() called.

Code in a `resize` handler should never rely on the number of times the handler is called. Depending on implementation, the `resize` events can be sent continuously as the resizing is in progress (the typical behavior in Internet Explorer and WebKit-based browsers such as Safari and Chrome), or only once at the end of the resize operation (the typical behavior in Firefox).

.scroll()

Bind an event handler to the `scroll` JavaScript event, or trigger that event on an element.

```
.scroll(handler)
.scroll()
```

Parameters (first version)

- `handler`: A function to execute each time the event is triggered

Return value

The jQuery object, for chaining purposes.

Description

This method is a shortcut for `.bind('scroll', handler)` in the first variation, and `.trigger('scroll')` in the second.

The `scroll` event is sent to an element when the user scrolls to a different place in the element. It applies to `window` objects as well as to scrollable frames and elements with the `overflow` CSS property set to `scroll` (or `auto` when the element's explicit height is less than the height of its contents).

For example, consider the following HTML code:

```
<div id="target"
    style="overflow: scroll; width: 200px; height: 100px;">
  Lorem ipsum dolor sit amet, consectetur adipisicing elit,
  sed do eiusmod tempor incididunt ut labore et dolore magna
  aliqua. Ut enim ad minim veniam, quis nostrud exercitation
  ullamco laboris nisi ut aliquip ex ea commodo consequat.
  Duis aute irure dolor in reprehenderit in voluptate velit
  esse cillum dolore eu fugiat nulla pariatur. Excepteur
  sint occaecat cupidatat non proident, sunt in culpa qui
  officia deserunt mollit anim id est laborum.
</div>
<div id="other">
  Trigger the handler
</div>
```

The style definition is present to make the target element small enough to
be scrollable.

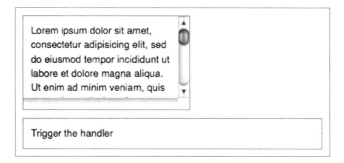

The `scroll` event handler can be bound to this element.

```
$('#target').scroll(function() {
  $.print('Handler for .scroll() called.');
});
```

Now when the user scrolls the text up or down, the following message is displayed:

Handler for .scroll() called.

We can trigger the event manually when another element is clicked.

```
$('#other').click(function() {
  $('#target').scroll();
});
```

After this code executes, clicks on **Trigger the handler** will also display the
same message.

A `scroll` event is sent whenever the element's scroll position changes, regardless
of the cause. Clicking on or dragging the scroll bar, dragging inside the element,
pressing the arrow keys, or scrolling the mouse wheel could cause this event.

6

Effect Methods

The jQuery library provides several techniques for adding animation to a web page. These include simple, standard animations that are frequently used and the ability to craft sophisticated custom **effects**. In this chapter, we'll closely examine each of the effect methods, revealing all of the mechanisms jQuery has for providing visual feedback to the user.

 Some of the examples in this chapter use the `$.print()` function to print results to the page. This is a simple plug-in, which will be discussed in Chapter 10, *Plug-in API*.

Pre-packaged effects

These methods allow us to quickly apply commonly-used effects with a minimum of configuration.

.show()

Display the matched elements.

```
.show([duration] [, callback])
```

Parameters

- `duration` (optional): A string or number determining how long the animation will run
- `callback` (optional): A function to call once the animation is complete

Return value

The jQuery object, for chaining purposes.

Description

With no parameters, the `.show()` method is the simplest way to display an element.

```
$('.target').show();
```

The matched elements will be revealed immediately with no animation. This is roughly equivalent to calling `.css('display', 'block')`, except that the `display` property is restored to whatever it was initially. If an element has a `display` value of `inline`, then is hidden and shown, it will once again be displayed `inline`.

When a duration is provided, `.show()` becomes an animation method. The `.show()` method animates the width, height, and opacity of the matched elements simultaneously.

Durations are given in milliseconds; higher values indicate slower animations, not faster ones. The `'fast'` and `'slow'` strings can be supplied to indicate durations of `200` and `600` milliseconds, respectively.

If supplied, the callback is fired once the animation is complete. This can be useful for stringing different animations together in sequence. The callback is not sent any arguments, but `this` is set to the DOM element being animated. If multiple elements are animated, it is important to note that the callback is executed once per matched element, not once for the animation as a whole.

We can animate any element, such as a simple image:

```
<div id="clickme">
  Click here
</div>
<img id="book" src="book.png" alt="" width="100" height="123" />
```

With the element initially hidden, we can show it slowly.

```
$('#clickme').click(function() {
  $('#book').show('slow', function() {
    $.print('Animation complete.');
  });
});
```

.hide()

Hide the matched elements.

```
.hide([duration][, callback])
```

Parameters

- `duration` (optional): A string or number determining how long the animation will run
- `callback` (optional): A function to call once the animation is complete

Return value

The jQuery object, for chaining purposes.

Description

With no parameters, the `.hide()` method is the simplest way to hide an element.

```
$('.target').hide();
```

The matched elements will be hidden immediately, with no animation. This is roughly equivalent to calling `.css('display', 'none')`, except that the value of the `display` property is saved in jQuery's data cache so that `display` can later be restored to its initial value. If an element has a `display` value of `inline`, and then is hidden and shown, it will once again be displayed `inline`.

When a duration is provided, `.hide()` becomes an animation method. The `.hide()` method animates the width, height, and opacity of the matched elements simultaneously. When these properties reach 0, the `display` style property is set to `none` to ensure that the element no longer affects the layout of the page.

Durations are given in milliseconds; higher values indicate slower animations, not faster ones. The `'fast'` and `'slow'` strings can be supplied to indicate durations of `200` and `600` milliseconds, respectively.

If supplied, the callback is fired once the animation is complete. This can be useful for stringing different animations together in sequence. The callback is not sent any arguments, but `this` is set to the DOM element being animated. If multiple elements are animated, it is important to note that the callback is executed once per matched element, not once for the animation as a whole.

We can animate any element, such as a simple image:

```
<div id="clickme">
  Click here
</div>
<img id="book" src="book.png" alt="" width="100" height="123" />
```

With the element initially shown, we can hide it slowly.

```
$('#clickme').click(function() {
  $('#book').hide('slow', function() {
    $.print('Animation complete.');
  });
});
```

.toggle()

Display or hide the matched elements.

```
.toggle([duration][, callback])
.toggle(showOrHide)
```

Parameters (first version)

- `duration` (optional): A string or number determining how long the animation will run

- `callback` (optional): A function to call once the animation is complete

Parameters (second version)

- `showOrHide`: A Boolean indicating whether to show or hide the elements

Return value

The jQuery object, for chaining purposes.

Description

With no parameters, the `.toggle()` method simply toggles the visibility of elements:

```
$('.target').toggle();
```

The matched elements will be revealed or hidden immediately with no animation. If the element is initially displayed, it will be hidden; if hidden, it will be shown. The `display` property is saved and restored as needed. If an element has a `display` value of `inline`, then is hidden and shown, it will once again be displayed `inline`.

When a duration is provided, `.toggle()` becomes an animation method. The `.toggle()` method animates the width, height, and opacity of the matched elements simultaneously. When these properties reach 0 after a hiding animation, the `display` style property is set to `none` to ensure that the element no longer affects the layout of the page.

Durations are given in milliseconds; higher values indicate slower animations, not faster ones. The `'fast'` and `'slow'` strings can be supplied to indicate durations of `200` and `600` milliseconds, respectively.

If supplied, the callback is fired once the animation is complete. This can be useful for stringing different animations together in sequence. The callback is not sent any arguments, but this is set to the DOM element being animated. If multiple elements are animated, it is important to note that the callback is executed once per matched element, not once for the animation as a whole.

We can animate any element, such as a simple image:

```
<div id="clickme">
  Click here
</div>
<img id="book" src="book.png" alt="" width="100" height="123" />
```

We will cause .toggle() to be called when another element is clicked.

```
$('#clickme').click(function() {
  $('#book').toggle('slow', function() {
    $.print('Animation complete.');
  });
});
```

With the element initially shown, we can hide it slowly with the first click:

A second click will show the element once again:

The second version of the method accepts a Boolean parameter. If this parameter is `true`, then the matched elements are shown; if `false`, the elements are hidden. In essence, the following statement

```
$('#foo').toggle(showOrHide);
```

is equivalent to:

```
if (showOrHide) {
  $('#foo').show();
}
else {
  $('#foo').hide();
}
```

 There is also an event method named `.toggle()`.
For details on this method, see Chapter 5, *Event Methods*.

.slideDown()

Display the matched elements with a sliding motion.
`.slideDown([duration] [, callback])`

Parameters

- `duration` (optional): A string or number determining how long the animation will run
- `callback` (optional): A function to call once the animation is complete

Return value

The jQuery object, for chaining purposes.

Description

The `.slideDown()` method animates the height of the matched elements. This causes lower parts of the page to slide down, making way for the revealed items.

Durations are given in milliseconds; higher values indicate slower animations, not faster ones. The `'fast'` and `'slow'` strings can be supplied to indicate durations of `200` and `600` milliseconds, respectively. If any other string is supplied, or if the `duration` parameter is omitted, the default duration of `400` milliseconds is used.

If supplied, the callback is fired once the animation is complete. This can be useful for stringing different animations together in sequence. The callback is not sent any arguments, but `this` is set to the DOM element being animated. If multiple elements are animated, it is important to note that the callback is executed once per matched element, not once for the animation as a whole.

We can animate any element, such as a simple image:

```
<div id="clickme">
  Click here
</div>
<img id="book" src="book.png" alt="" width="100" height="123" />
```

With the element initially hidden, we can show it slowly.

```
$('#clickme').click(function() {
  $('#book').slideDown('slow', function() {
    $.print('Animation complete.');
  });
});
```

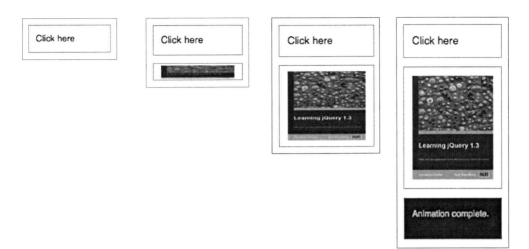

.slideUp()

Hide the matched elements with a sliding motion.

```
.slideUp([duration] [, callback])
```

Parameters

- `duration` (optional): A string or number determining how long the animation will run
- `callback` (optional): A function to call once the animation is complete

Return value

The jQuery object, for chaining purposes.

Description

The `.slideUp()` method animates the height of the matched elements. This causes lower parts of the page to slide up, appearing to conceal the items. Once the height reaches 0, the `display` style property is set to `none` to ensure that the element no longer affects the layout of the page.

Durations are given in milliseconds; higher values indicate slower animations, not faster ones. The `'fast'` and `'slow'` strings can be supplied to indicate durations of `200` and `600` milliseconds, respectively. If any other string is supplied, or if the `duration` parameter is omitted, the default duration of `400` milliseconds is used.

If supplied, the callback is fired once the animation is complete. This can be useful for stringing different animations together in sequence. The callback is not sent any arguments, but this is set to the DOM element being animated. If multiple elements are animated, it is important to note that the callback is executed once per matched element, not once for the animation as a whole.

We can animate any element, such as a simple image:

```
<div id="clickme">
  Click here
</div>
<img id="book" src="book.png" alt="" width="100" height="123" />
```

With the element initially shown, we can hide it slowly.

```
$('#clickme').click(function() {
  $('#book').slideUp('slow', function() {
    $.print('Animation complete.');
  });
});
```

.slideToggle()

Display or hide the matched elements with a sliding motion.

```
.slideToggle([duration] [, callback])
```

Parameters

- `duration` (optional): A string or number determining how long the animation will run
- `callback` (optional): A function to call once the animation is complete

Return value

The jQuery object, for chaining purposes.

Description

The `.slideToggle()` method animates the height of the matched elements. This causes lower parts of the page to slide up or down, appearing to reveal or conceal the items. If the element is initially displayed, it will be hidden; if hidden, it will be shown. The `display` property is saved and restored as needed. If an element has a `display` value of `inline`, then is hidden and shown, it will once again be displayed `inline`. When the height reaches 0 after a hiding animation, the `display` style property is set to `none` to ensure that the element no longer affects the layout of the page.

Durations are given in milliseconds; higher values indicate slower animations, not faster ones. The `'fast'` and `'slow'` strings can be supplied to indicate durations of `200` and `600` milliseconds, respectively.

If supplied, the callback is fired once the animation is complete. This can be useful for stringing different animations together in sequence. The callback is not sent any arguments, but `this` is set to the DOM element being animated. If multiple elements are animated, it is important to note that the callback is executed once per matched element, not once for the animation as a whole.

We can animate any element, such as a simple image:

```
<div id="clickme">
  Click here
</div>
<img id="book" src="book.png" alt="" width="100" height="123" />
```

We will cause `.slideToggle()` to be called when another element is clicked.

```
$('#clickme').click(function() {
  $('#book').slideToggle('slow', function() {
    $.print('Animation complete.');
  });
});
```

With the element initially shown, we can hide it slowly with the first click:

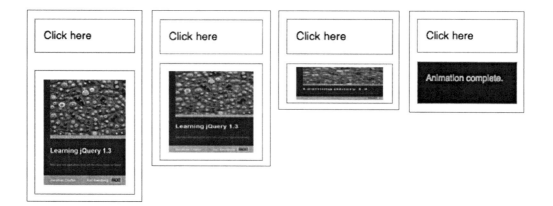

A second click will show the element once again:

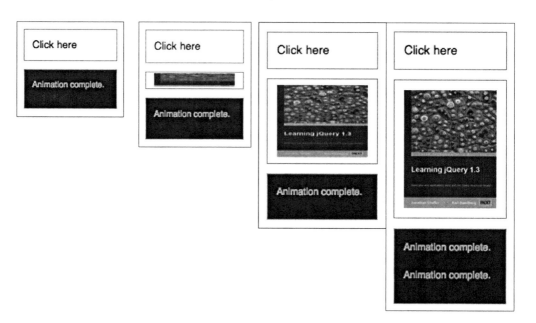

.fadeIn()

Display the matched elements by fading them to opaque.

```
.fadeIn([duration][, callback])
```

Parameters

- `duration` (optional): A string or number determining how long the animation will run
- `callback` (optional): A function to call once the animation is complete

Return value

The jQuery object, for chaining purposes.

Description

The `.fadeIn()` method animates the opacity of the matched elements.

Durations are given in milliseconds; higher values indicate slower animations, not faster ones. The `'fast'` and `'slow'` strings can be supplied to indicate durations of `200` and `600` milliseconds, respectively. If any other string is supplied, or if the `duration` parameter is omitted, the default duration of `400` milliseconds is used.

If supplied, the callback is fired once the animation is complete. This can be useful for stringing different animations together in sequence. The callback is not sent any arguments, but `this` is set to the DOM element being animated. If multiple elements are animated, it is important to note that the callback is executed once per matched element, not once for the animation as a whole.

We can animate any element, such as a simple image:

```
<div id="clickme">
  Click here
</div>
<img id="book" src="book.png" alt="" width="100" height="123" />
```

With the element initially hidden, we can show it slowly.

```
$('#clickme').click(function() {
  $('#book').fadeIn('slow', function() {
    $.print('Animation complete.');
  });
});
```

.fadeOut()

Hide the matched elements by fading them to transparent.
.fadeOut([duration] [, callback])

Parameters

- duration (optional): A string or number determining how long the animation will run

- callback (optional): A function to call once the animation is complete

Return value

The jQuery object, for chaining purposes.

Description

The .fadeOut() method animates the opacity of the matched elements. Once the opacity reaches 0, the display style property is set to none, so the element no longer affects the layout of the page.

Durations are given in milliseconds; higher values indicate slower animations, not faster ones. The 'fast' and 'slow' strings can be supplied to indicate durations of 200 and 600 milliseconds, respectively. If any other string is supplied, or if the duration parameter is omitted, the default duration of 400 milliseconds is used.

If supplied, the callback is fired once the animation is complete. This can be useful for stringing different animations together in sequence. The callback is not sent any arguments, but this is set to the DOM element being animated. If multiple elements are animated, it is important to note that the callback is executed once per matched element, not once for the animation as a whole.

We can animate any element, such as a simple image:

```
<div id="clickme">
  Click here
</div>
<img id="book" src="book.png" alt="" width="100" height="123" />
```

With the element initially shown, we can hide it slowly.

```
$('#clickme').click(function() {
  $('#book').fadeOut('slow', function() {
    $.print('Animation complete.');
  });
});
```

.fadeTo()

Adjust the opacity of the matched elements.
```
.fadeTo(duration, opacity[, callback])
```

Parameters

- `duration`: A string or number determining how long the animation will run
- `opacity`: A number between 0 and 1 denoting the target opacity
- `callback` (optional): A function to call once the animation is complete

Return value

The jQuery object, for chaining purposes.

Description

The `.fadeTo()` method animates the opacity of the matched elements.

Durations are given in milliseconds; higher values indicate slower animations, not faster ones. The `'fast'` and `'slow'` strings can be supplied to indicate durations of `200` and `600` milliseconds, respectively. If any other string is supplied, the default duration of `400` milliseconds is used. Unlike the other effect methods, `.fadeTo()` requires that `duration` be explicitly specified.

If supplied, the callback is fired once the animation is complete. This can be useful for stringing different animations together in sequence. The callback is not sent any arguments, but `this` is set to the DOM element being animated. If multiple elements are animated, it is important to note that the callback is executed once per matched element, not once for the animation as a whole.

We can animate any element, such as a simple image:

```
<div id="clickme">
  Click here
</div>
<img id="book" src="book.png" alt="" width="100" height="123" />
```

With the element initially shown, we can dim it slowly.

```
$('#clickme').click(function() {
  $('#book').fadeTo('slow', 0.5, function() {
    $.print('Animation complete.');
  });
});
```

With `duration` set to `0`, this method just changes the `opacity` CSS property, so `.fadeTo(0, opacity)` is the same as `.css('opacity', opacity)`.

Customized effects

This section describes how to create effects that are not provided out of the box by jQuery.

.animate()

Perform a custom animation of a set of CSS properties.

```
.animate(properties[, duration][, easing][, callback])
.animate(properties, options)
```

Parameters (first version)

- `properties`: A map of CSS properties that the animation will move toward
- `duration` (optional): A string or number determining how long the animation will run
- `easing` (optional): A string indicating which easing function to use for the transition
- `callback` (optional): A function to call once the animation is complete

Parameters (second version)

- `properties`: A map of CSS properties that the animation will move toward
- `options`: A map of additional options to pass to the method. Supported keys are:
    - `duration`: A string or number determining how long the animation will run
    - `easing`: A string indicating which easing function to use for the transition
    - `complete`: A function to call once the animation is complete
    - `step`: A function to be called after each step of the animation
    - `queue`: A Boolean indicating whether to place the animation in the effects queue. If `false`, the animation will begin immediately
    - `specialEasing`: A map of one or more of the CSS properties defined by the `properties` argument and their corresponding easing functions

Return value

The jQuery object, for chaining purposes.

Description

The `.animate()` method allows us to create animation effects on any numeric CSS property. The only required parameter is a map of CSS properties. This map is similar to the one that can be sent to the `.css()` method, except that the range of properties is more restrictive.

All animated properties are treated as a number of pixels, unless otherwise specified. The units `em` and `%` can be specified where applicable.

In addition to numeric values, each property can take the strings `'show'`, `'hide'`, and `'toggle'`. These shortcuts allow for custom hiding and showing animations that take into account the display type of the element.

Animated properties can also be **relative**. If a value is supplied with a leading `+=` or `-=` sequence of characters, then the target value is computed by adding or subtracting the given number to or from the current value of the property.

Durations are given in milliseconds; higher values indicate slower animations, not faster ones. The `'fast'` and `'slow'` strings can be supplied to indicate durations of `200` and `600` milliseconds, respectively. Unlike the other effect methods, `.fadeTo()` requires that `duration` be explicitly specified.

If supplied, the callback is fired once the animation is complete. This can be useful for stringing different animations together in sequence. The callback is not sent any arguments, but this is set to the DOM element being animated. If multiple elements are animated, it is important to note that the callback is executed once per matched element, not once for the animation as a whole.

We can animate any element, such as a simple image:

```
<div id="clickme">
  Click here
</div>
<img id="book" src="book.png" alt="" width="100" height="123"
  style="position: relative; left: 10px;" />
```

We can animate the opacity, left offset, and height of the image simultaneously.

```
$('#clickme').click(function() {
  $('#book').animate({
    opacity: 0.25,
    left: '+=50',
    height: 'toggle'
  }, 5000, function() {
    $.print('Animation complete.');
  });
});
```

  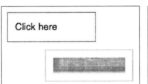

Note that we have specified `toggle` as the target value of the `height` property. As the image was visible before, the animation shrinks the height to 0 to hide it. A second click then reverses this transition:

The `opacity` of the image is already at its target value, so this property is not animated by the second click. As we specified the target value for `left` as a relative value, the image moves even farther to the right during this second animation.

The `position` attribute of the element must not be `static` if we wish to animate the `left` property as we do in the example.

> The jQuery UI project extends the `.animate()` method by allowing some non-numeric styles, such as colors, to be animated. The project also includes mechanisms for specifying animations through CSS classes rather than individual attributes.

The remaining parameter of .animate() is a string naming an **easing function** to use. An easing function specifies the speed at which the animation progresses at different points within the animation. The only easing implementations in the jQuery library are the default, called swing, and one that progresses at a constant pace, called linear. More easing functions are available with the use of plug-ins, most notably the jQuery UI suite.

As of jQuery version 1.4, we can set per-property easing functions within a single .animate() call. In the first version of .animate(), each property can take an array as its value: The first member of the array is the CSS property and the second member is an easing function. If a per-property easing function is not defined for a particular property, it uses the value of the .animate() method's optional easing argument. If the easing argument is not defined, the default swing function is used.

We can simultaneously animate the width and height with the swing easing function and the opacity with the linear easing function:

```
$('#clickme').click(function() {
  $('#book').animate({
    width: ['toggle', 'swing'],
    height: ['toggle', 'swing'],
    opacity: 'toggle'
  }, 5000, 'linear', function() {
    $.print('Animation complete.');
  });
});
```

In the second version of .animate(), the options map can include the specialEasing property, which is itself a map of CSS properties and their corresponding easing functions. We can simultaneously animate the width using the linear easing function and the height using the easeOutBounce easing function.

```
$('#clickme').click(function() {
  $('#book').animate({
    width: 'toggle',
    height: 'toggle'
  }, {
    duration: 5000,
    specialEasing: {
      width: 'linear',
      height: 'easeOutBounce'
    },
    complete: function() {
      $.print('Animation complete.');
    }
  });
});
```

As previously noted, a plug-in is required for the easeOutBounce function.

.stop()

Stop the currently running animation on the matched elements.

```
.stop([clearQueue] [, jumpToEnd])
```

Parameters

- `clearQueue` (optional): A Boolean indicating whether to remove queued animation as well. Defaults to `false`
- `jumpToEnd` (optional): A Boolean indicating whether to complete the current animation immediately. Defaults to `false`

Return value

The jQuery object, for chaining purposes.

Description

When `.stop()` is called on an element, the currently running animation (if any) is immediately stopped. For instance, if an element is being hidden with `.slideUp()` when `.stop()` is called, the element will now still be displayed, but will be a fraction of its previous height. Callback functions are not called.

If more than one animation method is called on the same element, the later animations are placed in the **effects queue** for the element. These animations will not begin until the first one completes. When `.stop()` is called, the next animation in the queue begins immediately. If the `clearQueue` parameter is provided with a value of `true`, then the rest of the animations in the queue are removed and never run.

If the `jumpToEnd` property is provided with a value of `true`, the current animation stops, but the element is immediately given its target values for each CSS property. In our `.slideUp()` example, the element would be immediately hidden. The callback function is then immediately called, if provided.

The usefulness of the `.stop()` method is evident when we need to animate an element on `mouseenter` and `mouseleave`.

```
<div id="hoverme">
  Hover me
  <img id="hoverme" src="book.png" alt="" width="100" height="123" />
</div>
```

We can create a nice fade effect without the common problem of multiple queued animations by adding `.stop(true, true)` to the chain.

```
$('#hoverme-stop-2').hover(function() {
  $(this).find('img').stop(true, true).fadeOut();
}, function() {
  $(this).find('img').stop(true, true).fadeIn();
});
```

 Animations may be stopped globally by setting the `$.fx.off` property to `true`. When this is done, all animation methods will immediately set elements to their final state when called, rather than displaying an effect.

.delay()

Set a timer to delay execution of subsequent items in the queue.

`.delay(duration, [queueName])`

Parameters

- `duration`: An integer indicating the number of milliseconds to delay execution of the next item in the queue

- `queueName` (optional): A string containing the name of the queue. Defaults to `fx`, the standard effects queue

Return value

The jQuery object, for chaining purposes.

Description

Added to jQuery in version 1.4, the `.delay()` method allows us to delay the execution of functions that follow it in the queue. It can be used with the standard effects queue or with a custom queue.

Using the standard effects queue, we can, for example, set an 800-millisecond delay between the `.slideUp()` and `.fadeIn()` of the `foo` element:

```
$('#foo').slideUp(300).delay(800).fadeIn(400);
```

When this statement is executed, the element slides up for `300` milliseconds and then pauses for `800` milliseconds before fading in for `400` milliseconds.

.queue()

Manipulate the queue of functions to be executed on the matched elements.

```
.queue([queueName])
.queue([queueName], newQueue)
.queue([queueName], callback)
```

Parameters (first version)

- queueName (optional): A string containing the name of the queue. Defaults to fx, the standard effects queue

Parameters (second version)

- queueName (optional): A string containing the name of the queue. Defaults to fx, the standard effects queue
- newQueue: An array of functions to replace the current queue contents

Parameters (third version)

- queueName (optional): A string containing the name of the queue. Defaults to fx, the standard effects queue
- callback: The new function to add to the queue

Return value (first version)

An array of the functions currently in the first element's queue.

Return value (second and third versions)

The jQuery object, for chaining purposes.

Description

Every element can have one or many queues of functions attached to it by jQuery. In most applications, only one queue (called fx) is used. Queues allow a sequence of actions to be called on an element asynchronously, without halting program execution. The typical example of this is calling multiple animation methods on an element. For example:

```
$('#foo').slideUp().fadeIn();
```

When this statement is executed, the element begins its sliding animation immediately, but the fading transition is placed on the fx queue to be called only once the sliding transition is complete.

The `.queue()` method allows us to directly manipulate this queue of functions. The first and second versions of the function allow us to retrieve the entire array of functions or replace it with a new array, respectively.

The third version allows us to place a new function at the end of the queue. This feature is similar to providing a callback function with an animation method, but does not require the callback to be given at the time the animation is performed.

```
$('#foo').slideUp();
$('#foo').queue(function() {
  $.print('Animation complete.');
  $(this).dequeue();
});
```

This is equivalent to:

```
$('#foo').slideUp(function() {
  $.print('Animation complete.');
});
```

Note that when adding a function with `.queue()`, we should ensure that `.dequeue()` is eventually called so that the next function in line executes.

.dequeue()

Execute the next function on the queue for the matched elements.

```
.dequeue([queueName])
```

Parameters

- `queueName` (optional): A string containing the name of the queue. Defaults to `fx`, the standard effects queue

Return value

The jQuery object, for chaining purposes.

Description

When `.dequeue()` is called, the next function on the queue is removed from the queue and then executed. This function should, in turn (directly or indirectly), cause `.dequeue()` to be called so that the sequence can continue.

.clearQueue()

Remove from the queue all items that have not yet been run.

        .clearQueue([queueName])

Parameter

- queueName (optional): A string containing the name of the queue. Defaults to fx, the standard effects queue

Return value

The jQuery object, for chaining purposes.

Description

When the .clearQueue() method is called, all functions on the queue that have not been executed are removed from the queue. When used without an argument, .clearQueue() removes the remaining functions from fx, the standard effects queue. In this way it is similar to .stop(true). However, while the .stop() method is meant to be used only with animations, .clearQueue() can also be used to remove any function that has been added to a generic jQuery queue with the .queue() method.

7
AJAX Methods

The jQuery library has a full suite of AJAX capabilities. The functions and methods therein allow us to load data from the server without a browser page refresh. In this chapter, we'll examine each of the available AJAX methods and functions. We'll see various ways of initiating an AJAX request, as well as several methods that can observe the requests that are in progress at any time.

 Some of the examples in this chapter use the $.print() function to print results to the page. This is a simple plug-in, which will be discussed in Chapter 10, *Plug-in API*.

Low-level interface

These methods can be used to make arbitrary AJAX requests.

$.ajax()

Perform an asynchronous HTTP (AJAX) request.
```
$.ajax(settings)
```

Parameters

- settings: A map of options for the request. It can contain the following items:
    - url: A string containing the URL to which the request is sent.
    - async (optional): A Boolean indicating whether to perform the request asynchronously. Defaults to true.

- ° `beforeSend` (optional): A callback function that is executed before the request is sent.

- ° `cache` (optional): A Boolean indicating whether to allow the browser to cache the response. Defaults to `true`.

- ° `complete` (optional): A callback function that executes whenever the request finishes.

- ° `contentType` (optional): A string containing a MIME content type to set for the request. Defaults to `application/x-www-form-urlencoded`.

- ° `context` (optional): An object (typically a DOM element) to set as `this` within the callback functions. Defaults to `window`. New in jQuery 1.4.

- ° `data` (optional): A map or string that is sent to the server with the request.

- ° `dataFilter` (optional): A callback function that can be used to preprocess the response data before passing it to the `success` handler.

- ° `dataType` (optional): A string defining the type of data expected back from the server (`xml`, `html`, `json`, `jsonp`, `script`, or `text`).

- ° `error` (optional): A callback function that is executed if the request fails.

- ° `global` (optional): A Boolean indicating whether global AJAX event handlers will be triggered by this request. Defaults to `true`.

- ° `ifModified` (optional): A Boolean indicating whether the server should check if the page is modified before responding to the request. Defaults to `false`.

- ° `jsonp` (optional): A string containing the name of the JSONP parameter to be passed to the server. Defaults to `callback`.

- ° `password` (optional): A string containing a password to be used when responding to an HTTP authentication challenge.

- ° `processData` (optional): A Boolean indicating whether to convert submitted data from object form into query string form. Defaults to `true`.

- ° `scriptCharset` (optional): A string indicating the character set of the data being fetched; only used when the `dataType` parameter is `jsonp` or `script`.

- ° success (optional): A callback function that is executed if the request succeeds.

- ° timeout (optional): A number of milliseconds after which the request will time out in failure.

- ° type (optional): A string defining the HTTP method to use for the request, such as GET or POST. Defaults to GET.

- ° username (optional): A string containing a user name to be used when responding to an HTTP authentication challenge.

- ° xhr (optional): A callback function that is used to create the XMLHttpRequest object. Defaults to a browser-specific implementation.

Return value

The XMLHttpRequest object that was created, if any.

Description

The $.ajax() function underlies all AJAX requests sent by jQuery. It is rarely necessary to directly call this function, as several higher-level alternatives such as $.get() and .load() are available and are easier to use. However, if less common options are required, $.ajax() can be used more flexibly.

At its simplest, the $.ajax() function must at least specify a URL from which to load the data.

```
$.ajax({
  url: 'ajax/test.html',
});
```

 Even this sole required parameter may be made optional by setting a default using the $.ajaxSetup() function.

Using the only required option, this example loads the contents of the specified URL; but does nothing with the result. To use the result, we can implement one of the callback functions.

Callback functions

The beforeSend, error, dataFilter, success, and complete options all take callback functions that are invoked at the appropriate times.

- beforeSend is called before the request is sent, and is passed the XMLHttpRequest object as a parameter.

- error is called if the request fails. It is passed the XMLHttpRequest object, a string indicating the error type, and an exception object if applicable.

- dataFilter is called on success. It is passed the returned data and the value of dataType, and must return the (possibly altered) data to pass on to success.

- success is called if the request succeeds. It is passed the returned data, as well as a string containing the success code.

- complete is called when the request is finished, whether in failure or success. It is passed the XMLHttpRequest object, as well as a string containing the success or error code.

To make use of the returned HTML, we can implement a success handler as follows:

```
$.ajax({
  url: 'ajax/test.html',
  success: function(data) {
    $('.result').html(data);
    $.print('Load was performed.');
  }
});
```

Such a simple example would generally be better served by using .load() or $.get().

Data types

The $.ajax() function relies on the server to provide information about the retrieved data. If the server reports the return data as XML, the result can be traversed using normal XML methods or jQuery's selectors. If another type is detected, such as HTML in the preceding example, the data is treated as text.

Different data handling can be achieved by using the dataType option. Besides plain xml, the dataType can be html, json, jsonp, script, or text.

The text and xml types return the data with no processing. The data is simply passed on to the success handler, either through the responseText or responseHTML property of the XMLHttpRequest object, respectively.

We must ensure that the MIME type reported by the web server matches our choice of `dataType`. In particular, XML must be declared by the server as `text/xml` or `application/xml` for consistent results.

If `html` is specified, any embedded JavaScript inside the retrieved data is executed before the HTML is returned as a string. Similarly, `script` will execute the JavaScript that is pulled back from the server, and then return the script itself as textual data.

The `json` type parses the fetched data file as a JavaScript object and returns the constructed object as the result data. To do so, it uses `JSON.parse()` when the browser supports it; otherwise it uses a `Function` **constructor**. JSON data is convenient for communicating structured data in a way that is concise and easy for JavaScript to parse. If the fetched data file exists on a remote server, the `jsonp` type can be used instead. This type will cause a query string parameter of `callback=?` to be appended to the URL; the server should prepend the JSON data with the callback name to form a valid JSONP response. If a specific parameter name is desired instead of `callback`, it can be specified with the `jsonp` option to `$.ajax()`.

 A detailed description of the JSONP protocol is beyond the scope of this reference guide. This protocol is an extension of the JSON format, requiring some server-side code to detect and handle the query string parameter. Comprehensive treatments can be found online, or in Chapter 7 of the book *Learning jQuery 1.3*.

When data is retrieved from remote servers (which is only possible using the `script` or `jsonp` data types), the operation is performed using a `<script>` tag rather than an `XMLHttpRequest` object. In this case, no `XMLHttpRequest` object is returned from `$.ajax()`, nor is one passed to the handler functions such as `beforeSend`.

Sending data to the server

By default, AJAX requests are sent using the GET HTTP method. If the POST method is required, the method can be specified by setting a value for the `type` option. This option affects how the contents of the `data` option are sent to the server.

The `data` option can contain either a query string of the form `key1=value1&key2=value2`, or a map of the form `{key1: 'value1', key2: 'value2'}`. If the latter form is used, the data is converted into a query string before it is sent. This processing can be circumvented by setting `processData` to `false`. The processing might be undesirable if we wish to send an XML object to the server. In this case, we would also want to change the `contentType` option from `application/x-www-form-urlencoded` to a more appropriate MIME type.

Advanced options

The `global` option prevents handlers registered using `.ajaxSend()`, `.ajaxError()`, and similar methods from firing when this request would trigger them. For example, this can be useful to suppress a loading indicator that we implemented with `.ajaxSend()` if the requests are frequent and brief. See the *Descriptions* of these methods for more details.

If the server performs HTTP authentication before providing a response, the user name and password pair can be sent via the `username` and `password` options.

AJAX requests are time-limited, so errors can be caught and handled to provide a better user experience. Request timeouts are usually either left at their default, or set as a global default using `$.ajaxSetup()`, rather than being overridden for specific requests with the `timeout` option.

By default, requests are always issued, but the browser may serve results out of its cache. To disallow use of the cached results, set `cache` to `false`. Set `ifModified` to `true` to cause the request to report failure if the asset has not been modified since the last request.

The `scriptCharset` allows the character set to be explicitly specified for requests that use a `<script>` tag (that is, a type of `script` or `jsonp`). This is useful if the script and host page have differing character sets.

The first letter in AJAX stands for "asynchronous," meaning that the operation occurs in parallel and the order of completion is not guaranteed. The `async` option to `$.ajax()` defaults to `true`, indicating that code execution can continue after the request is made. Setting this option to `false` (and thus making the call no longer asynchronous) is strongly discouraged, as it can cause the browser to become unresponsive.

 Rather than making requests synchronous using this option, better results can be had using the **blockUI** plug-in. For more information on using plug-ins, see Chapter 10, *Plug-in API*.

The `$.ajax()` function returns the `XMLHttpRequest` object that it creates. Normally, jQuery handles the creation of this object internally, but a custom function for manufacturing one can be specified using the `xhr` option. The returned object can generally be discarded, but it does provide a lower-level interface for observing and manipulating the request. In particular, calling `.abort()` on the object will halt the request before it completes.

$.ajaxSetup()

> Set default values for future AJAX requests.
>
> ```
> $.ajaxSetup(settings)
> ```

Parameters

- `settings`: A map of options for future requests; same possible items as in `$.ajax()`

Return value

None

Description

For details on the settings available for `$.ajaxSetup()`, see `$.ajax()`.

All subsequent AJAX calls using any function will use the new settings, unless overridden by the individual calls, until the next invocation of `$.ajaxSetup()`.

For example, we could set a default for the URL parameter before pinging the server repeatedly as follows:

```
$.ajaxSetup({
  url: 'ping.php'
});
```

Now each time an AJAX request is made, this URL will be used automatically.

```
$.ajax({});
$.ajax({
  data: {'date': Date()}
});
```

Global callback functions should be set with their respective global AJAX event handler methods — `.ajaxStart()`, `.ajaxStop()`, `.ajaxComplete()`, `.ajaxError()`, `.ajaxSuccess()`, and `.ajaxSend()` — rather than within the `settings` object for `$.ajaxSetup()`.

Shorthand methods

These methods perform the more common types of AJAX requests in less code.

$.get()

> Load data from the server using a GET HTTP request.
>
> ```
> $.get(url[, data][, success][, dataType])
> ```

Parameters

- `url`: A string containing the URL to which the request is sent
- `data` (optional): A map or string that is sent to the server with the request
- `success` (optional): A callback function that is executed if the request succeeds
- `dataType` (optional): A string defining the type of data expected back from the server (`xml`, `html`, `json`, `jsonp`, `script`, or `text`)

Return value

The `XMLHttpRequest` object that was created.

Description

This is a shorthand AJAX function, which is equivalent to the following:

```
$.ajax({
  url: url,
  data: data,
  success: success,
  dataType: dataType
});
```

The callback is passed the returned data, which will be an XML root element, text string, JavaScript file, or JSON object, depending on the MIME type of the response.

Most implementations will specify a success handler.

```
$.get('ajax/test.html', function(data) {
  $('.result').html(data);
  $.print('Load was performed.');
});
```

This example fetches the requested HTML snippet and inserts it on the page.

.load()

Load data from the server and place the returned HTML into the matched element.

```
.load(url[, data] [, success])
```

Parameters

- `url`: A string containing the URL to which the request is sent
- `data` (optional): A map or string that is sent to the server with the request
- `success` (optional): A callback function that is executed if the request succeeds

Return value

The jQuery object, for chaining purposes.

Description

This method is the simplest way to fetch data from the server. It is roughly equivalent to `$.get(url, data, success)`, except that it is a method rather than global function and has an implicit callback function. When a successful response is detected, `.load()` sets the HTML contents of the matched element to the returned data. This means that most uses of the method can be quite simple, for example:

```
$('.result').load('ajax/test.html');
```

The provided callback, if any, is executed after this post-processing has been performed:

```
$('.result').load('ajax/test.html', function() {
  $.print('Load was performed.');
});
```

The POST method is used if data is provided as an object; otherwise, GET is assumed.

 The event handling suite also has a method named `.load()`. Which one is fired depends on the set of arguments passed.

Loading page fragments

The .load() method, unlike $.get(), allows only part of a remote document to be fetched. This is achieved with a special syntax for the url parameter. If one or more space characters are included in the string, the portion of the string following the first space is assumed to be a jQuery selector. This selector is used to identify a portion of the remote document to retrieve.

We could modify the preceding example to fetch only part of the document as follows:

```
$('.result').load('ajax/test.html #container');
```

When this method executes, the content of ajax/test.html is loaded, but then jQuery parses this returned document to find the element with an ID of container. The inner content of this element is inserted into the element with a class of result and the rest of the loaded document is discarded.

$.post()

> Load data from the server using a POST HTTP request.
> ```
> $.post(url[, data][, success][, dataType])
> ```

Parameters

- url: A string containing the URL to which the request is sent
- data (optional): A map or string that is sent to the server with the request
- success (optional): A callback function that is executed if the request succeeds
- dataType (optional): A string defining the type of data expected back from the server (xml, html, json, jsonp, script, or text)

Return value

The XMLHttpRequest object that was created.

Description

This is a shorthand AJAX function, which is equivalent to the following:

```
$.ajax({
  type: 'POST',
  url: url,
  data: data,
```

```
  success: success,
  dataType: dataType
});
```

The callback is passed the returned data, which will be an XML root element or a text string depending on the MIME type of the response.

Most implementations will specify a success handler.

```
$.post('ajax/test.html', function(data) {
  $('.result').html(data);
  $.print('Load was performed.');
});
```

This example fetches the requested HTML snippet and inserts it on the page.

Pages fetched with POST are never cached, so the cache and ifModified options have no effect on these requests.

$.getJSON()

Load JSON-encoded data from the server using a GET HTTP request.
```
$.getJSON(url[, data][, success])
```

Parameters

- url: A string containing the URL to which the request is sent
- data (optional): A map or string that is sent to the server with the request
- success (optional): A callback function that is executed if the request succeeds

Return value

The XMLHttpRequest object that was created.

Description

This is a shorthand AJAX function, which is equivalent to the following:

```
$.ajax({
  url: url,
  dataType: 'json',
  data: data,
  success: success
});
```

The callback is passed the returned data, which will be a JavaScript object or array as defined by the JSON structure and parsed using `JSON.parse()` or a Function constructor.

 For details on the JSON format, see `http://json.org/`.

Most implementations will specify a success handler.

```
$.getJSON('ajax/test.json', function(data) {
   $('.result').html('<p>' + data.foo + '</p>'
      + '<p>' + data.baz[1] + '</p>');
   $.print('Load was performed.');
});
```

This example, of course, relies on the structure of the JSON file.

```
{
   "foo": "The quick brown fox jumps over the lazy dog.",
   "bar": "ABCDEFG",
   "baz": [52, 97]
}
```

Using this structure, the example inserts the first string and second number from the file onto the page.

If there is a syntax error in the JSON file, the request will usually fail silently. Avoid frequent hand-editing of JSON data for this reason.

If the specified URL is on a remote server, the request is treated as JSONP instead. See the *Description* of the `jsonp` data type in *$.ajax()* for more details.

$.getScript()

Load a JavaScript file from the server using a GET HTTP request, then execute it.

```
$.getScript(url[, success])
```

Parameters

- `url`: A string containing the URL to which the request is sent
- `success` (optional): A callback function that is executed if the request succeeds

Return value

The `XMLHttpRequest` object that was created.

Description

This is a shorthand AJAX function, which is equivalent to the following:

```
$.ajax({
  url: url,
  type: 'script',
  success: success
});
```

The callback is passed the returned JavaScript file. This is generally not useful as the script will already have run at this point.

The script is executed in the global context, so it can refer to other variables and use jQuery functions. Included scripts should have some impact on the current page.

```
$('.result').html('<p>Lorem ipsum dolor sit amet.</p>');
```

The script can then be included and run by referencing the file name as follows:

```
$.getScript('ajax/test.js', function() {
  $.print('Load was performed.');
});
```

Global AJAX event handlers

These methods register handlers to be called when certain events, such as initialization or completion, take place for any AJAX request on the page.

.ajaxComplete()

> Register a handler to be called when AJAX requests complete.
>   `.ajaxComplete(handler)`

Parameters

- `handler`: The function to be invoked

Return value

The jQuery object, for chaining purposes.

Description

Whenever an AJAX request completes, jQuery triggers the `ajaxComplete` event. Any and all handlers that have been registered with the `.ajaxComplete()` method are executed at this time.

To observe this method in action, we can set up a basic AJAX load request as follows:

```
<div class="trigger">Trigger</div>
<div class="result"></div>
<div class="log"></div>
```

We can attach our event handler to any element.

```
$('.log').ajaxComplete(function() {
  $(this).text('Triggered ajaxComplete handler.');
});
```

Now, we can make an AJAX request using any jQuery method.

```
$('.trigger').click(function() {
  $('.result').load('ajax/test.html');
});
```

When the user clicks the button and the AJAX request completes, the log message is displayed.

 As `.ajaxComplete()` is implemented as a method rather than a global function, we can use the `this` keyword as we do here to refer to the selected elements within the callback function.

All `ajaxComplete` handlers are invoked, regardless of what AJAX request was completed. If we must differentiate between the requests, we can use the parameters passed to the handler. Each time an `ajaxComplete` handler is executed, it is passed the event object, the `XMLHttpRequest` object, and the settings object that was used in the creation of the request. We can restrict our callback to only handling events dealing with a particular URL, for example:

```
$('.log').ajaxComplete(function(e, xhr, settings) {
  if (settings.url == 'ajax/test.html') {
    $(this).text('Triggered ajaxComplete handler.');
  }
});
```

.ajaxError()

Register a handler to be called when AJAX requests complete with an error.

```
.ajaxError(handler)
```

Parameters

- `handler`: The function to be invoked

Return value

The jQuery object, for chaining purposes.

Description

Whenever an AJAX request completes with an error, jQuery triggers the `ajaxError` event. Any and all handlers that have been registered with the `.ajaxError()` method are executed at this time.

To observe this method in action, we can set up a basic AJAX load request as follows:

```
<div class="trigger">Trigger</div>
<div class="result"></div>
<div class="log"></div>
```

We can attach our event handler to any element.

```
$('.log').ajaxError(function() {
  $(this).text('Triggered ajaxError handler.');
});
```

Now, we can make an AJAX request using any jQuery method.

```
$('.trigger').click(function() {
  $('.result').load('ajax/missing.html');
});
```

The log message is displayed when the user clicks the button and the AJAX request fails because the requested file is missing.

 As `.ajaxError()` is implemented as a method rather than a global function, we can use the `this` keyword as we do here to refer to the selected elements within the callback function.

All `ajaxError` handlers are invoked, regardless of what AJAX request was completed. If we must differentiate between the requests, we can use the parameters passed to the handler. Each time an `ajaxError` handler is executed, it is passed the event object, the `XMLHttpRequest` object, and the settings object that was used in the creation of the request. If the request failed because JavaScript raised an exception, the exception object is passed to the handler as a fourth parameter. We can restrict our callback to only handling events dealing with a particular URL, for example:

```
$('.log').ajaxError(function(e, xhr, settings, exception) {
  if (settings.url == 'ajax/missing.html') {
    $(this).text('Triggered ajaxError handler.');
  }
});
```

.ajaxSend()

> Register a handler to be called when AJAX requests are begun.
>   `.ajaxSend(handler)`

Parameters

- `handler`: The function to be invoked

Return value

The jQuery object, for chaining purposes.

Description

Whenever an AJAX request is about to be sent, jQuery triggers the `ajaxSend` event. Any and all handlers that have been registered with the `.ajaxSend()` method are executed at this time.

To observe this method in action, we can set up a basic AJAX load request as follows:

```
<div class="trigger">Trigger</div>
<div class="result"></div>
<div class="log"></div>
```

We can attach our event handler to any element.

```
$('.log').ajaxSend(function() {
  $(this).text('Triggered ajaxSend handler.');
});
```

Now, we can make an AJAX request using any jQuery method.

```
$('.trigger').click(function() {
  $('.result').load('ajax/test.html');
});
```

When the user clicks the button and the AJAX request is about to begin, the log message is displayed.

 As .ajaxSend() is implemented as a method rather than a global function, we can use the this keyword as we do here to refer to the selected elements within the callback function.

All ajaxSend handlers are invoked, regardless of what AJAX request is to be sent. If we must differentiate between the requests, we can use the parameters passed to the handler. Each time an ajaxSend handler is executed, it is passed the event object, the XMLHttpRequest object, and the settings object that was used in the creation of the request. We can restrict our callback to only handling events dealing with a particular URL, for example:

```
$('.log').ajaxSend(function(e, xhr, settings) {
  if (settings.url == 'ajax/test.html') {
    $(this).text('Triggered ajaxSend handler.');
  }
});
```

.ajaxStart()

Register a handler to be called when the first AJAX request begins.

.ajaxStart(handler)

Parameters

- handler: The function to be invoked

Return value

The jQuery object, for chaining purposes.

Description

Whenever an AJAX request is about to be sent, jQuery checks whether there are any other outstanding AJAX requests. If none are in progress, jQuery triggers the `ajaxStart` event. Any and all handlers that have been registered with the `.ajaxStart()` method are executed at this time.

To observe this method in action, we can set up a basic AJAX load request as follows:

```
<div class="trigger">Trigger</div>
<div class="result"></div>
<div class="log"></div>
```

We can attach our event handler to any element.

```
$('.log').ajaxStart(function() {
  $(this).text('Triggered ajaxStart handler.');
});
```

Now, we can make an AJAX request using any jQuery method.

```
$('.trigger').click(function() {
  $('.result').load('ajax/test.html');
});
```

The log message is displayed when the user clicks the button and the AJAX request is sent.

 As `.ajaxStart()` is implemented as a method rather than a global function, we can use the `this` keyword as we do here to refer to the selected elements within the callback function.

.ajaxStop()

Register a handler to be called when all AJAX requests have completed.
```
.ajaxStop(handler)
```

Parameters

- `handler`: The function to be invoked

Return value

The jQuery object, for chaining purposes.

Description

Whenever an AJAX request completes, jQuery checks whether there are any other outstanding AJAX requests. If none remain, jQuery triggers the ajaxStop event. Any and all handlers that have been registered with the .ajaxStop() method are executed at this time.

To observe this method in action, we can set up a basic AJAX load request as follows:

```
<div class="trigger">Trigger</div>
<div class="result"></div>
<div class="log"></div>
```

We can attach our event handler to any element.

```
$('.log').ajaxStop(function() {
  $(this).text('Triggered ajaxStop handler.');
});
```

Now, we can make an AJAX request using any jQuery method.

```
$('.trigger').click(function() {
  $('.result').load('ajax/test.html');
});
```

The log message is displayed when the user clicks the button and the AJAX request completes.

> As .ajaxStop() is implemented as a method rather than a global function, we can use the this keyword as we do here to refer to the selected elements within the callback function.

.ajaxSuccess()

Register a handler to be called when AJAX requests complete and are successful.
.ajaxSuccess(handler)

Parameters

- handler: The function to be invoked

Return value

The jQuery object, for chaining purposes.

Description

Whenever an AJAX request completes successfully, jQuery triggers the `ajaxSuccess` event. Any and all handlers that have been registered with the `.ajaxSuccess()` method are executed at this time.

To observe this method in action, we can set up a basic AJAX load request as follows:

```
<div class="trigger">Trigger</div>
<div class="result"></div>
<div class="log"></div>
```

We can attach our event handler to any element.

```
$('.log').ajaxSuccess(function() {
  $(this).text('Triggered ajaxSuccess handler.');
});
```

Now, we can make an AJAX request using any jQuery method.

```
$('.trigger').click(function() {
  $('.result').load('ajax/test.html');
});
```

The log message is displayed when the user clicks the button and the AJAX request completes.

 As `.ajaxSuccess()` is implemented as a method rather than a global function, we can use the `this` keyword as we do here to refer to the selected elements within the callback function.

All `ajaxSuccess` handlers are invoked, regardless of what AJAX request was completed. If we must differentiate between the requests, we can use the parameters passed to the handler. Each time an `ajaxSuccess` handler is executed, it is passed the event object, the `XMLHttpRequest` object, and the settings object that was used in the creation of the request. We can restrict our callback to only handling events dealing with a particular URL, for example:

```
$('.log').ajaxSuccess(function(e, xhr, settings) {
  if (settings.url == 'ajax/test.html') {
    $(this).text('Triggered ajaxSuccess handler.');
  }
});
```

Helper functions

These functions assist with common idioms encountered when performing AJAX tasks.

.serialize()

Encode a set of form elements as a string for submission.
```
.serialize()
```

Parameters

None

Return value

A string containing the serialized representation of the elements.

Description

The .serialize() method creates a text string in a standard URL-encoded notation. It operates on a jQuery object representing a set of form elements. The form elements can be of several types.

```
<form>
  <div><input type="text" name="a" value="1" id="a" /></div>
  <div><input type="text" name="b" value="2" id="b" /></div>
  <div><input type="hidden" name="c" value="3" id="c" /></div>
  <div>
    <textarea name="d" rows="8" cols="40">4</textarea>
  </div>
  <div><select name="e">
    <option value="5" selected="selected">5</option>
    <option value="6">6</option>
    <option value="7">7</option>
  </select></div>
  <div>
    <input type="checkbox" name="f" value="8" id="f" />
  </div>
  <div>
    <input type="submit" name="g" value="Submit" id="g" />
  </div>
</form>
```

The `.serialize()` method can act on a jQuery object that has selected individual form elements, such as `<input>`, `<textarea>`, and `<select>`. However, it is typically easier to select the `<form>` tag itself for serialization.

```
$('form').submit(function() {
  $.print($(this).serialize());
  return false;
});
```

This produces a standard-looking query string as follows:

```
a=1&b=2&c=3&d=4&e=5
```

.serializeArray()

Encode a set of form elements as an array of names and values.
```
    .serializeArray()
```

Parameters

None

Return value

An array of objects containing the serialized representation of each element.

Description

The `.serializeArray()` method creates a JavaScript array of objects, ready to be encoded as a JSON string. It operates on a jQuery object representing a set of form elements. The form elements can be of several types.

```
<form>
  <div><input type="text" name="a" value="1" id="a" /></div>
  <div><input type="text" name="b" value="2" id="b" /></div>
  <div><input type="hidden" name="c" value="3" id="c" /></div>
  <div>
    <textarea name="d" rows="8" cols="40">4</textarea>
  </div>
  <div><select name="e">
    <option value="5" selected="selected">5</option>
    <option value="6">6</option>
    <option value="7">7</option>
  </select></div>
  <div>
```

```
      <input type="checkbox" name="f" value="8" id="f" />
    </div>
    <div>
      <input type="submit" name="g" value="Submit" id="g" />
    </div>
</form>
```

The .serializeArray() method can act on a jQuery object that has selected individual form elements, such as <input>, <textarea>, and <select>. However, it is typically easier to select the <form> tag itself for serialization.

```
$('form').submit(function() {
  $.print($(this).serializeArray());
  return false;
});
```

This produces the following data structure:

```
[
  {
    name: a
    value: 1
  },
  {
    name: b
    value: 2
  },
  {
    name: c
    value: 3
  },
  {
    name: d
    value: 4
  },
  {
    name: e
    value: 5
  }
]
```

8
Miscellaneous Methods

In the preceding chapters, we have examined many categories of jQuery methods. However, a few methods provided by the library have so far defied categorization. In this final method reference chapter, we will explore these remaining methods that can be used to abbreviate common JavaScript idioms.

 Some of the examples in this chapter use the $.print() function to print results to the page. This is a simple plug-in, which will be discussed in Chapter 10, *Plug-in API*.

Setup methods

These functions are useful before the main code body begins.

$.noConflict()

Relinquish jQuery's control of the $ variable.

```
$.noConflict([removeAll])
```

Parameters

- removeAll (optional): A Boolean indicating whether to remove all jQuery variables from the global scope (including jQuery itself)

Return value

The global jQuery object. This can be set to a variable to provide an alternative shortcut to $.

Description

Many JavaScript libraries use $ as a function or variable name, just as jQuery does. In jQuery's case, $ is just an alias for jQuery. So, all functionality is available without using $. If we need to use another JavaScript library alongside jQuery, we can return control of $ back to the other library with a call to $.noConflict().

```
<script type="text/javascript" src="other_lib.js"></script>
<script type="text/javascript" src="jquery.js"></script>
<script type="text/javascript">
  $.noConflict();
  // Code that uses other library's $ can follow here.
</script>
```

This technique is especially effective in conjunction with the .ready() method's ability to alias the jQuery object, as within any callback passed to .ready(), we can use $ if we wish, without fear of conflicts later.

```
<script type="text/javascript" src="other_lib.js"></script>
<script type="text/javascript" src="jquery.js"></script>
<script type="text/javascript">
  $.noConflict();
  jQuery(document).ready(function($) {
    // Code that uses jQuery's $ can follow here.
  });
  // Code that uses other library's $ can follow here.
</script>
```

If necessary, we can free up the jQuery name as well by passing true as an argument to the method. This is rarely necessary and if we must do this (for example, if we need to use multiple versions of the jQuery library on the same page), we need to consider that most plug-ins rely on the presence of the jQuery variable and may not operate correctly in this situation.

DOM element methods

These methods help us to work with the DOM elements underlying each jQuery object.

.size()

Return the number of DOM elements matched by the jQuery object.
```
.size()
```

Return value

The number of elements matched.

Description

Suppose we had a simple unordered list on the page:

```
<ul>
  <li>foo</li>
  <li>bar</li>
</ul>
```

We could determine the number of list items by calling `.size()`.

```
$.print('Size: ' + $('li').size());
```

This would output the count of items:

Size: 2

 The `.length` property, discussed in Chapter 9, *jQuery Properties*, is a slightly faster way to get this information.

.get()

Retrieve the DOM elements matched by the jQuery object.

```
.get([index])
```

Parameters

- `index` (optional): An integer indicating which element to retrieve

Return value

A DOM element or an array of DOM elements if the index is omitted.

Description

The `.get()` method grants us access to the DOM nodes underlying each jQuery object. Suppose we had a simple unordered list on the page:

```
<ul>
  <li id="foo">foo</li>
  <li id="bar">bar</li>
</ul>
```

Without a parameter, `.get()` returns all of the elements.

```
$.print($('li').get());
```

All of the matched DOM nodes are returned by this call, contained in a standard array:

[<li id="foo">, <li id="bar">]

With an index specified, `.get()` will retrieve a single element.

```
$.print($('li').get(0));
```

As the index is zero-based, the first list item is returned:

<li id="foo">

Each jQuery object also masquerades as an array, so we can use the array-dereferencing operator to get at the list item instead.

```
$.print($('li')[0]);
```

However, this syntax lacks some of the additional capabilities of `.get()`, such as specifying a negative index.

```
$.print($('li').get(-1));
```

A negative index is counted from the end of the matched set. So this example will return the last item in the list:

<li id="bar">

.index()

Search for a given element from among the matched elements.
```
.index()
.index(element)
.index(string)
```

Parameters (first version)
None

Return value (first version)
An integer indicating the position of the first element within the jQuery object relative to its sibling elements, or -1 if not found.

Parameters (second version)

- `element`: The DOM element or first element within the jQuery object to look for

Return value (second version)

An integer indicating the position of the element within the jQuery object, or `-1` if not found.

Parameters (third version)

- `string`: A selector representing a jQuery collection in which to look for an element

Return value (third version)

An integer indicating the position of the element within the jQuery object, or `-1` if not found.

Description

`.index()`, which is the complementary operation to `.get()` (which accepts an index and returns a DOM node), can take a DOM node and returns an index. Suppose we had a simple unordered list on the page:

```
<ul>
  <li id="foo">foo</li>
  <li id="bar">bar</li>
  <li id="baz">baz</li>
</ul>
```

If we have retrieved one of the three list items (for example, through a DOM function or as the context to an event handler), `.index()` can search for this list item within the set of matched elements:

```
var listItem = document.getElementById('bar');
$.print('Index: ' + $('li').index(listItem));
```

We get back the zero-based position of the list item:

Index: 1

Similarly, if we have retrieved a jQuery object consisting of one of the three list items, `.index()` will search for that list item.

```
var listItem = $('#bar');
$.print('Index: ' + $('li').index(listItem));
```

We get back the zero-based position of the list item:

Index: 1

Note that if the jQuery collection — used as the `.index()` method's argument — contains more than one element, the first element within the matched set of elements will be used.

```
var listItems = $('li:gt(0)');
$.print('Index: ' + $('li').index(listItems));
```

We get back the zero-based position of the first list item within the matched set:

Index: 1

If we use a string as the `.index()` method's argument, it is interpreted as a jQuery selector string. The first element among the object's matched elements that also matches this selector is located.

```
var listItem = $('#bar');
$.print('Index: ' + listItem.index('li'));
```

We get back the zero-based position of the list item:

Index: 1

If we omit the argument, `.index()` will return the position of the first element within the set of matched elements in relation to its siblings.

```
$.print('Index: ' + $('#bar').index();
```

Again, we get back the zero-based position of the list item:

Index: 1

Collection manipulation

These helper functions manipulate arrays, maps, and strings.

.each()

Iterate over a collection, firing a callback function on each item.

```
.each(callback)
$.each(collection, callback)
```

Parameters (first version)

- `callback`: A function to execute for each matched element

Return value (first version)

The jQuery object, for chaining purposes.

Parameters (second version)

- `collection`: An object or array to iterate over
- `callback`: A function to execute for each item in the collection

Return value (second version)

The `collection` argument.

Description

The `.each()` method and `$.each()` function are designed to make looping constructs concise and less error-prone. They iterate over a collection, executing a callback function once for every item in that collection.

The first syntax listed earlier is a method of jQuery objects and when called, it iterates over the DOM elements that are part of the object. Each time the callback runs, it is passed the current loop iteration, beginning from 0. More importantly, the callback is fired in the context of the current DOM element, so the `this` keyword refers to the element.

Suppose we had a simple unordered list on the page:

```
<ul>
  <li>foo</li>
  <li>bar</li>
</ul>
```

We could select the list items and iterate across them.

```
$('li').each(function(index) {
  $.print(index + ': ' + $(this).text());
});
```

A message is thus logged for each item in the list:

0: foo

1: bar

The second syntax is similar, but it is a global function rather than a method. The collection is passed as the first parameter in this case, and can be either a map (JavaScript object) or an array. In the case of an array, the callback is passed an array index and a corresponding array value each time.

```
$.each([52, 97], function(key, value) {
  $.print(key + ': ' + value);
});
```

This produces two messages:

0: 52

1: 97

If a map is used as the collection, the callback is passed a key-value pair each time.

```
var map = {
  'flammable': 'inflammable',
  'duh': 'no duh'
};
$.each(map, function(index, value) {
  $.print(index + ': ' + value);
});
```

Once again, this produces two messages:

flammable: inflammable

duh: no duh

We can stop the loop from within the callback function by returning `false`.

$.grep()

> Winnow an array down to a selected set of items.
> ```
> $.grep(array, filter[, invert])
> ```

Parameters

- `array`: An array to search through
- `filter`: A function to apply as a test for each item
- `invert` (optional): A Boolean indicating whether to reverse the filter condition

Return value

The newly constructed, filtered array.

Description

The `$.grep()` method removes items from an array as necessary so that all remaining items pass a provided test. The test is a function that is passed an array item and the index of the item within the array. Only if the test returns `true` will the item be in the result array.

As is typical with jQuery methods, the callback function is often defined anonymously.

```
var array = [0, 1, 52, 97];
$.print(array);
array = $.grep(array, function(item) {
  return (item > 50);
});
$.print(array);
```

All array **items that** are over 50 are preserved in the result array:

[0, 1, 52, 97]

[52, 97]

We can **invert this test** by adding the third parameter.

```
var array = [0, 1, 52, 97];
$.print(array);
array = $.grep(array, function(item) {
  return (item > 50);
}, true);
$.print(array);
```

This now produces an array of items less than or equal to 50:

[0, 1, 52, 97]

[0, 1]

$.makeArray()

Convert an array-like object into a true JavaScript array.

```
$.makeArray(obj)
```

Parameters

- `obj`: The object to convert to an array

Return value

The newly constructed array.

Description

Many methods, both in jQuery and in JavaScript in general, return objects that are array-like. For example, the jQuery factory function `$()` returns a jQuery object that has many of the properties of an array (a `length`, the `[]` array access operator, and so on), but is not exactly the same as an array and lacks some of an array's built-in methods (such as `.pop()` and `.reverse()`).

The `$.makeArray()` function allows us to convert such an object into a native array.

```
var obj = $('li');
$.print(obj);

obj = $.makeArray(obj);
$.print(obj);
```

The function call turns the numerically indexed object into an array:

{0: <li>, 1: <li>}

[<li>, <li>]

Note that after the conversion, any special features the object had (such as the jQuery methods in our example) will no longer be present. The object is now a plain array.

$.inArray()

Search for a specified value within an array.
```
$.inArray(value, array)
```

Parameters

- `value`: The value to search for
- `array`: An array through which to search

Return value

An integer indicating the position of the element within an array, or `-1` if not found.

Description

The $.inArray() method is similar to JavaScript's native .indexOf() method in that it returns -1 when it doesn't find a match. If the first element within the array matches value, $.inArray() returns 0.

As JavaScript treats 0 as loosely equal to false (that is, 0 == false, but 0 !== false), if we're checking for the presence of value within array, we need to check if it's not equal to (or greater than) -1.

```
var array = [0, 1, 52, 97];
$.print(array);
var inArray = $.inArray(0, array);
$.print(inArray);
$.print(inArray == true);
$.print(inArray > -1);
```

Note that as 0 is the first element in the array, it returns 0:

[0, 1, 52, 97]

0

false

true

$.map()

Transform an array into another one by using a transformation function.
```
$.map(array, transform)
```

Parameters

- array: The array to convert
- transform: A function to apply to each item

Return value

The newly constructed, transformed array.

Description

The $.map() method applies a function to each item in an array and collects the results into a new array. The transformation is a function that is passed an array item and the index of the item within the array.

As is typical with jQuery methods, the callback function is often defined anonymously.

```
var array = [0, 1, 52, 97];
$.print(array);
array = $.map(array, function(a) {
  return (a - 45);
});
$.print(array);
```

All array items are reduced by 45 in the result array:

[0, 1, 52, 97]

[-45, -44, 7, 52]

We can remove items from the array by returning `null` from the transformation function.

```
var array = [0, 1, 52, 97];
$.print(array);
array = $.map(array, function(a) {
  return (a > 50 ? a - 45 : null);
});
$.print(array);
```

This now produces an array of the items that were greater than 50, each reduced by 45:

[0, 1, 52, 97]

[7, 52]

If the transformation function returns an array rather than a scalar, the returned arrays are concatenated together to form the result.

```
var array = [0, 1, 52, 97];
$.print(array);
array = $.map(array, function(a, i) {
  return [a - 45, i];
});
$.print(array);
```

Instead of a two-dimensional result array, the map forms a flattened one:

[0, 1, 52, 97]

[-45, 0, -44, 1, 7, 2, 52, 3]

To perform this type of operation on a jQuery object rather than an array, use the `.map()` method, described in Chapter 3, *DOM Traversal Methods*.

$.merge()

> Merge the contents of two arrays together into the first array.
>
> ```
> $.merge(array1, array2)
> ```

Parameters

- `array1`: The first array to merge
- `array2`: The second array to merge

Return value

An array consisting of elements from both supplied arrays.

Description

The `$.merge()` operation forms an array that contains all elements from the two arrays. The orders of items in the arrays are preserved, with items from the second array appended.

```
var array1 = [0, 1, 52];
var array2 = [52, 97];
$.print(array1);
$.print(array2);
array = $.merge(array1, array2);
$.print(array);
```

The resulting array contains all five items:

[0, 1, 52]

[52, 97]

[0, 1, 52, 52, 97]

The $.merge() function is destructive. It alters the first parameter to add the items from the second. If you need the original first array, make a copy of it before calling $.merge(). Fortunately, $.merge() itself can be used for this duplication as follows:

```
var newArray = $.merge([], oldArray);
```

This shortcut creates a new, empty array and merges the contents of oldArray into it, effectively cloning the array.

$.unique()

> Create a copy of an array of DOM elements with the duplicates removed.
> $.unique(array)

Parameters

* array: An array of DOM elements

Return value

An array consisting of only unique objects.

Description

The $.unique() function searches through an array of objects, forming a new array that does not contain duplicate objects. This function only works on plain JavaScript arrays of DOM elements, and is chiefly used internally by jQuery.

$.extend()

> Merge the contents of two objects together into the first object.
> $.extend([recursive,][target,]properties
>   [, propertiesN])

Parameters

* recursive (optional): A Boolean indicating whether to merge objects within objects
* target (optional): An object that will receive the new properties
* properties: An object containing additional properties to merge in
* propertiesN: Additional objects containing properties to merge in

Return value

The target object after it has been modified.

Description

The `$.extend()` function merges two objects in the same way that `$.merge()` merges arrays. The properties of the second object are added to the first, creating an object with all the properties of both objects.

```
var object1 = {
  apple: 0,
  banana: {weight: 52, price: 100},
  cherry: 97
};
var object2 = {
  banana: {price: 200},
  durian: 100
};

$.print(object1);
$.print(object2);
var object = $.extend(object1, object2);
$.print(object);
```

The value for `durian` in the second object gets added to the first, and the value for `banana` gets overwritten:

{apple: 0, banana: {weight: 52, price: 100}, cherry: 97}

{banana: {price: 200}, durian: 100}

{apple: 0, banana: {price: 200}, cherry: 97, durian: 100}

The `$.extend()` function is destructive; the target object is modified in the process. This is generally desirable behavior, as `$.extend()` can in this way be used to simulate object inheritance. Methods added to the object become available to all code that has a reference to the object. However, if we want to preserve both of the original objects, we can do this by passing an empty object as the target.

```
var object = $.extend({}, object1, object2)
```

We can also supply more than two objects to `$.extend()`. In this case, properties from all of the objects are added to the target object.

If only one argument is supplied to $.extend(), this means the target argument was omitted. In this case, the jQuery object itself is assumed to be the target. By doing this, we can add new functions to the jQuery namespace. We will explore this capability when discussing how to create jQuery plug-ins.

The merge performed by $.extend() is not recursive by default. If a property of the first object is itself an object or array, it will be completely overwritten by a property with the same key in the second object. The values are not merged. This can be seen in the preceding example by examining the value of banana. However, by passing true for the first function argument, we can change this behavior.

```
var object = $.extend(true, object1, object2);
```

With this alteration, the weight property of banana is preserved while price is updated:

{apple: 0, banana: {weight: 52, price: 100}, cherry: 97}

{banana: {price: 200}, durian: 100}

{apple: 0, banana: {weight: 52, price: 200}, cherry: 97, durian: 100}

$.trim()

Remove whitespace from the ends of a string.
```
$.trim(string)
```

Parameters

- string: A string to trim

Return value

The trimmed string.

Description

The $.trim() function removes all newlines, spaces, and tabs from the beginning and end of the supplied string. If these whitespace characters occur in the middle of the string, they are preserved.

$.param()

Create a serialized representation of an object or array, suitable for use in a URL query string or AJAX request.

```
$.param(obj [, traditional])
```

Parameters

- `obj`: An object or an array of data to serialize

- `traditional` (optional): A Boolean indicating whether to perform a traditional "shallow" serialization of `obj`; defaults to `false`

Return value

A string containing the query string representation of the object.

Description

This function is used internally to convert form element values into a serialized string representation. See the *Description* of `.serialize()` in Chapter 7, *AJAX Methods* for more details.

As of jQuery 1.4, the `$.param()` method serializes deep objects recursively to accommodate modern scripting languages and frameworks such as PHP and Ruby on Rails.

 Because some frameworks have limited ability to parse serialized arrays, we should exercise caution when passing an `obj` argument that contains objects or arrays nested within another array.

We can display a query string representation of an object and a URI-decoded version of the same as follows:

```
var myObject = {
  a: {
    one: 1,
    two: 2,
    three: 3
  },
  b: [1,2,3]
};
var recursiveEncoded = $.param(myObject);
```

```
var recursiveDecoded = decodeURIComponent($.param(myObject));

$.print(recursiveEncoded);
$.print(recursiveDecoded);
```

The values of `recursiveEncoded` and `recursiveDecoded` are displayed as follows:

a%5Bone%5D=1&a%5Btwo%5D=2&a%5Bthree%5D=3&b%5B%5D=1&b%5B%5D=2&b%5B%5D=3

a[one]=1&a[two]=2&a[three]=3&b[]=1&b[]=2&b[]=3

To emulate the behavior of `$.param()` prior to jQuery 1.4, we can set the `traditional` argument to `true`:

```
var myObject = {
  a: {
    one: 1,
    two: 2,
    three: 3
  },
  b: [1,2,3]
};
var shallowEncoded = $.param(myObject, true);
var shallowDecoded = decodeURIComponent(shallowEncoded);

$.print(shallowEncoded);
$.print(shallowDecoded);
```

The values of `shallowEncoded` and `shallowDecoded` are displayed as follows:

a=%5Bobject+Object%5D&b=1&b=2&b=3

a=[object+Object]&b=1&b=2&b=3

Introspection

These methods allow us to determine the kind of data stored in a variable.

$.isArray()

Determine whether the argument is an array.

```
$.isArray(obj)
```

Parameters

- `obj`: The object to be tested

Return value

A Boolean indicating whether the object is a JavaScript array (not an array-like object, such as a jQuery object).

$.isFunction()

Determine whether the argument is a function object.
```
$.isFunction(obj)
```

Parameters

- `obj`: The object to be tested

Return value

A Boolean indicating whether the object is a function.

$.isPlainObject()

Determine whether the argument is a plain JavaScript object.
```
$.isPlainObject(obj)
```

Parameters

- `obj`: The object to be tested

Return value

A Boolean indicating whether the object is a plain JavaScript object (not an array or function, which are subclasses of `Object`).

$.isEmptyObject()

Determine whether the argument is an empty JavaScript object.
```
$.isEmptyObject(obj)
```

Parameters

- obj: The object to be tested

Return value

A Boolean indicating whether the object is an empty JavaScript object (that is, the object has no properties).

$.isXMLDoc()

> Determine whether the argument is an XML document.
>
> ```
> $.isXMLDoc(doc)
> ```

Parameters

- doc: The document to be tested

Return value

A Boolean indicating whether the document is an XML document (as opposed to an HTML document).

Data storage

These methods allow us to associate arbitrary data with specific DOM elements.

.data()

> Store or retrieve arbitrary data associated with the matched elements.
>
> ```
> .data(key, value)
> .data(obj)
> .data([key])
> ```

Parameters (first version)

- key: A string naming the piece of data to set
- value: The new data value

Return value (first version)

The jQuery object for chaining purposes.

Parameters (second version)

- `obj`: An object, of key-value pairs of data to set

Return value (second version)

The jQuery object, for chaining purposes.

Parameters (third version)

- `key` (optional): A string naming the piece of data to retrieve

Return value (third version)

The previously stored data.

Description

The `.data()` method allows us to attach data of any type to DOM elements in a way that is safe from circular references and, therefore, from memory leaks. We can set several distinct values for a single element and retrieve them one at a time, or as a set.

```
$('body').data('foo', 52);
$('body').data('bar', 'test');
$.print($('body').data('foo'));
$.print($('body').data());
```

The first two lines set values and the following two print them back out:

52

{foo: 52, bar: test}

As we see here, calling `.data()` with no parameters retrieves all of the values as a JavaScript object.

If we set an element's data using an object, all data previously stored with that element is overridden.

```
$('body').data('foo', 52);
$('body').data({one: 1, two: 2});
$.print($('body').data('foo'));
$.print($('body').data());
```

When lines one and two are printed out, we can see that the object in the second line writes over the `foo` data stored in the first line:

undefined

{one: 1, two: 2}

As the `foo` data no longer exists, line 3 displays its value as `undefined`.

.removeData()

Remove a previously stored piece of data.

    .removeData([key])

Parameters

- `key` (optional): A string naming the piece of data to delete

Return value

The jQuery object, for chaining purposes.

Description

The `.removeData()` method allows us to remove values that were previously set using `.data()`. When called with the name of a key, `.removeData()` deletes that particular value; when called with no arguments, all values are removed.

9
jQuery Properties

In addition to the many methods jQuery offers for interacting with the DOM and data, a number of properties are available for inspecting both the browser environment and individual jQuery objects.

 Some of the examples in this chapter use the $.print() function to print results to the page. This is a simple plug-in, which will be discussed in Chapter 10, *Plug-in API*.

Global properties

These properties are associated with the global jQuery object. They allow us to retrieve information about the user agent (web browser) that is executing the script and its features.

$.browser

> Information about the user agent displaying the page.

The $.browser property allows us to detect which web browser is accessing the page, as reported by the browser itself. It contains flags for each of the four most prevalent browser classes (Internet Explorer, Mozilla, Safari, and Opera) as well as version information.

```
$.print($.browser);
```

```
{
    version: 1.9.1.3,
    safari: false,
    opera: false,
    msie: false,
    mozilla: true
}
```

This property is available immediately. Therefore, it is safe to use it to determine whether to call `$(document).ready()` or not.

 The `$.browser` property is deprecated in jQuery 1.3, but there are no immediate plans to remove it.

As `$.browser` uses `navigator.useragent` to determine the platform, it is vulnerable to spoofing by the user or misrepresentation by the browser itself. It is always best to avoid browser-specific code entirely wherever possible. The `$.support` property is available for detection of support for particular features rather than relying on `$.browser`.

$.support

Information about the browser's support for specific rendering and JavaScript features.

Rather than using `$.browser` to detect the current user agent and alter the page presentation based on which browser is running, it is a good practice to perform **feature detection**. This means that prior to executing code that relies on a browser feature, we test to ensure that the feature works properly. To make this process simpler, jQuery performs many such tests and makes the results available to us as properties of the `$.support` object.

$.support.boxModel

This property is `true` if the current page has been rendered according to the specifications of the W3C CSS box model.

```
http://www.w3.org/TR/CSS2/box.html
```

$.support.cssFloat

This property is `true` if the name of the property containing the CSS `float` value is `.cssFloat`, as required by the Document Object Model CSS specification.

```
http://www.w3.org/TR/DOM-Level-2-Style/css.html#CSS-CSS2Properties-
cssFloat
```

$.support.hrefNormalized

This property is `true` if the `.getAttribute()` method retrieves the `href` attribute of elements unchanged, rather than normalizing it to a fully qualified URL.

```
http://www.w3.org/TR/DOM-Level-3-Core/core.html#ID-666EE0F9
```

$.support.htmlSerialize

This property is `true` if the browser is able to serialize/insert `<link>` elements using the `.innerHTML` property of elements.

```
http://www.w3.org/TR/2008/WD-html5-20080610/serializing.html#html-
fragment
```

$.support.leadingWhitespace

This property is `true` if the browser inserts content with `.innerHTML` exactly as provided; specifically, if leading whitespace characters are preserved.

```
http://www.w3.org/TR/2008/WD-html5-20080610/dom.html#innerhtml0
```

$.support.noCloneEvent

This property is `true` if cloned DOM elements are created without event handlers (that is, if the event handlers on the source element are not cloned).

```
http://www.w3.org/TR/DOM-Level-2-Events/events.html#Events-
Registration-interfaces-h3
```

$.support.objectAll

This property is `true` if the `.getElementsByTagName()` method returns all descendant elements when called with a wildcard argument (`'*'`).

```
http://www.w3.org/TR/WD-DOM/level-one-core.html#ID-745549614
```

$.support.opacity

This property is `true` if the browser respects the CSS property `opacity`.

`http://www.w3.org/TR/css3-color/#transparency`

$.support.scriptEval

This property is `true` if inline scripts are automatically evaluated and executed when inserted to the document using standard DOM manipulation methods, such as `.appendChild`.

`http://www.w3.org/TR/2008/WD-html5-20080610/tabular.html#script`

$.support.style

This property is `true` if inline styles for an element can be accessed through the DOM attribute called `style`, as required by the DOM Level 2 specification. In this case, `.getAttribute('style')` can retrieve this value; in Internet Explorer, `.cssText` is used for this purpose.

`http://www.w3.org/TR/DOM-Level-2-Style/css.html#CSS-ElementCSSInlineStyle`

$.support.tbody

This property is `true` if a `<table>` element can exist without a `<tbody>` element. According to the HTML specification, this subelement is optional, so the property should be `true` in a fully compliant browser. If `false`, we must account for the possibility of the browser injecting `<tbody>` tags implicitly.

`http://dev.w3.org/html5/spec/Overview.html#the-table-element`

jQuery object properties

Each jQuery object we create contains a number of properties alongside its methods. These properties allow us to inspect various attributes of the object.

.length

> The number of DOM elements matched by the jQuery object.

Suppose we had a simple unordered list on the page:

```
<ul>
  <li>foo</li>
  <li>bar</li>
</ul>
```

We can determine the number of list items by examining `.length`.

```
$.print('Length: ' + $('li').length);
```

This will output the count of items:

Length: 2

.selector

> The selector string that was used to create the jQuery object.

The `.live()` method for binding event handlers uses this property to determine how to perform its searches. Plug-ins that perform similar tasks may also find the property useful.

This property contains a string representing the matched set of elements. However, if DOM traversal methods have been called on the object, the string may not be a valid jQuery selector expression. For example, examine the value of the property on a newly-created jQuery object:

```
$.print($('ul li.foo').selector);
```

ul li.foo

Compare this with the value if the same elements are selected with a series of method calls:

```
$.print($('ul').find('li').filter('.foo').selector);
```

ul li.filter(.foo)

For this reason, the value of `.selector` is generally most useful immediately following the original creation of the object. Consequently, the `.live()` method should only be used in this scenario.

.context

> The DOM context that was used to create the jQuery object.

The `.live()` method for binding event handlers uses this property to determine the root element to use for its event delegation needs. Plug-ins that perform similar tasks may also find the property useful.

The value of this property is typically equal to `document`, as this is the default context for jQuery objects if none is supplied. The context may differ if, for example, the object was created by searching within an `<iframe>` or XML document.

10
The Plug-in API

Whenever a task is to be performed two or more times, it is a good idea to apply the **DRY** principle — **Don't Repeat Yourself**. To facilitate this, jQuery provides several tools for developers that go beyond simple iteration and function creation.

One of these powerful tools is jQuery's **plug-in** architecture, which makes creating and reusing extensions to the jQuery library a simple task. In this chapter, we'll take a brief look at using the existing third-party plug-ins and then delve into the various ways of extending jQuery with plug-ins that we define ourselves.

Using a plug-in

Taking advantage of an existing jQuery plug-in is very straightforward. A plug-in is contained in a standard JavaScript file. There are many ways to obtain the file, but the most straightforward way is to browse the jQuery plug-in repository at `http://plugins.jquery.com/`. The latest releases of many popular plug-ins are available for download from this site.

To make the methods of a plug-in available to us, we just include it in the `<head>` of the document. We must ensure that it appears *after* the main jQuery source file, and *before* our custom JavaScript code.

```
<head>
  <meta http-equiv="Content-Type"
    content="text/html; charset=utf-8"/>
  <script src="jquery.js" type="text/javascript"></script>
  <script src="jquery.plug-in.js"
    type="text/javascript"></script>
  <script src="custom.js" type="text/javascript"></script>
  <title>Example</title>
</head>
```

After that, we're ready to use any of the methods made public by the plug-in. For example, using the Form plug-in, we can add a single line inside our custom file's `$(document).ready()` method to make a form submit via AJAX.

```
$(document).ready(function() {
  $('#myForm').ajaxForm();
});
```

Each plug-in is independently documented. To find out more about other plug-ins, we can explore the documentation linked from the jQuery plug-in repository, or read the explanatory comments found in the source code itself.

If we can't find the answers to all of our questions in the plug-in repository, the author's web site, and the comments within the plug-in, we can always turn to the jQuery discussion list. Many of the plug-in authors are frequent contributors to the list and are willing to help with any problems that new users might face. Instructions for subscribing to the discussion list can be found at `http://docs.jquery.com/Discussion`.

 Appendix A, *Online Resources* lists even more resources for information about plug-ins and assistance in using them.

Developing a plug-in

As discussed earlier, plug-in development is a useful technique whenever we are going to perform a task more than once. Here we will itemize some of the components that can populate a plug-in file of our own design. Our plug-ins can use any combination of the following types of jQuery enhancements.

Object method

Add a new method to all jQuery objects created with the `$()` function.

```
jQuery.fn.methodName = methodDefinition;
```

Components

- `methodName`: A label for the new method
- `methodDefinition`: A function object to execute when `.methodName()` is called on a jQuery object instance

Description

When a function needs to act on one or more DOM elements, creating a new jQuery object method is usually appropriate. Object methods have access to the matched elements referenced by the jQuery object, and can inspect or manipulate them.

> When we add a method to `jQuery.fn`, we are actually adding it to the **prototype** of the `jQuery` object. Because of JavaScript's native **prototypal inheritance**, our method will apply to every **instance** of the jQuery object. For more information about prototypal inheritance, see `https://developer.mozilla.org/en/Core_JavaScript_1.5_Guide/Inheritance`.

The jQuery object can be retrieved from within the method implementation by referencing the `this` keyword. We can either call the built-in jQuery methods of this object, or we can extract the DOM nodes to work with them directly. As we saw in Chapter 8, *Miscellaneous Methods*, we can retrieve a referenced DOM node using array notation.

```
jQuery.fn.showAlert = function() {
  alert('You called the method on "' + this[0] + '".');
  return this;
}
```

However, we need to remember that a jQuery selector expression can always match zero, one, or multiple elements. We must allow for any of these scenarios when designing a plug-in method. The easiest way to accomplish this is to always call `.each()` on the method context. This enforces **implicit iteration**, which is important for maintaining consistency between plug-in and built-in methods. Within the function argument of the `.each()` call, `this` refers to each DOM element in turn.

```
jQuery.fn.showAlert = function() {
  this.each(function() {
    alert('You called the method on "' + this + '".');
  });
  return this;
}
```

Now we can apply our method to a jQuery object referencing multiple items.

```
$('.myClass').showAlert();
```

Our method produces a separate alert for each element that was matched by the preceding selector expression.

> **What is "this"?**
>
> It is very important to remember that the this keyword refers to
> different types of data in different situations. In the body of a plug-in
> method, this points to a jQuery object; in most callback functions such
> as .each() in our example, this points to a plain DOM element.

Note also that in these examples, we return the jQuery object itself (referenced by
this) when we are done with our work. This enables the **chaining** behavior that
jQuery users should be able to rely on. We must return a jQuery object from all
plug-in methods, unless the method is clearly intended to retrieve a different piece
of information and is documented as such.

A popular shorthand pattern for jQuery plug-ins is to combine the .each() iteration
and the return statement as follows:

```
jQuery.fn.showAlert = function() {
  return this.each(function() {
    alert('You called the method on "' + this + '".');
  });
}
```

This has the same effect as the previous code block—enforcing implicit iteration and
enabling chaining.

Global function

> Make a new function available to scripts contained within the jQuery namespace.
> ```
> jQuery.pluginName = fnDefinition;
> jQuery.extend({
>   pluginName: fnDefinition
> });
> jQuery.pluginName = {
>   function1: fnDefinition1,
>   function2: fnDefinition2
> };
> ```

Components (first and second versions)

- pluginName: The name of the current plug-in

- fnDefinition: A function object to execute when $.pluginName() is called

Components (third version)

- `pluginName`: The name of the current plug-in
- `function1`: A label for the first function
- `fnDefinition1`: A function object to execute when `$.pluginName.function1()` is called
- `function2`: A label for the second function
- `fnDefinition2`: A function object to execute when `$.pluginName.function2()` is called

Description

What we call **global functions** here are technically methods of the `jQuery` function object. Practically speaking, though, they are functions within a jQuery namespace. By placing the function within the jQuery namespace, we reduce the chance of name conflicts with other functions and variables in scripts.

Plug-ins with a single function

The first and second usages above illustrate the creation of a global function when the plug-in needs only a single function. By using the plug-in name as the function name, we can ensure that our function definition will not be trod on by other plug-ins (as long as the others follow the same guideline!). The new function is assigned as a property of the `jQuery` function object:

```
jQuery.myPlugin = function() {
   alert('This is a test. This is only a test.');
};
```

Now in any code that uses this plug-in, we can write:

```
jQuery.myPlugin();
```

We can also use the $ alias and write:

```
$.myPlugin();
```

This will work just like any other function call and the alert will be displayed.

Plug-ins with multiple functions

In the third usage, we see how to define global functions when more than one is needed by the same plug-in. We encapsulate all of the plug-ins within a single namespace named after our plug-in.

```
jQuery.myPlugin = {
   foo: function() {
     alert('This is a test. This is only a test.');
```

```
  },
  bar: function(param) {
    alert('This function was passed "' + param + '".');
  }
};
```

To invoke these functions, we address them as members of an object named after our plug-in, which is itself a property of the global jQuery function object.

```
$.myPlugin.foo();
$.myPlugin.bar('baz');
```

The functions are now properly protected from collisions with other functions and variables in the global namespace.

In general, it is wise to use this second usage from the start, even if it seems only one function will be needed, as it makes future expansion easier.

Example: A simple print function

In the various examples in the preceding reference chapters, we have had the need to output information to the screen to illustrate method behaviors. JavaScript's `alert()` function is often used for this type of demonstration, but does not allow for the frequent, timely messages we needed on occasion. A better alternative is the `console.log()` function available to Firefox and Safari, which allows printing messages to a separate log that does not interrupt the flow of interaction on the page. As this function is not available to Internet Explorer prior to version 8, we used a custom function to achieve this style of message logging.

The Firebug Lite script (described in Appendix B, *Development Tools*) provides a very robust cross-platform logging facility. The method we develop here is tailored specifically for the examples in the preceding chapters.

To print messages onto the screen, we are going to call the `$.print()` function. Implementing this function is simple as shown in the following code snippet:

```
jQuery.print = function(message) {
  var $output = jQuery('#print-output');

  if ($output.length === 0) {
    $output = jQuery('<div id="print-output" />')
      .appendTo('body');
  }
```

```
    jQuery('<div class="print-output-line" />')
      .html(message)
      .appendTo($output);
  };
```

Our function first determines whether a container exists for our messages. If no element with the `print-output` ID already exists, we create one and append it to the `<body>` element. Then, we make a new container for our message, place the message inside it, and append it to the `print-output` container.

Note that we use the `jQuery` identifier rather than `$` throughout the script to make sure the plug-in is safe in situations where `$.noConflict()` has been called.

Selector expression

> Add a new way to find DOM elements using a jQuery selector string.
> ```
> jQuery.extend(jQuery.expr[selectorType], {
>   selectorName: elementTest
> });
> ```

Components

- `selectorType`: The prefix character for the selector string, which indicates which type of selector is being defined. In practice, the useful value for plug-ins is `':'`, which indicates a pseudo-class selector.

- `selectorName`: A string uniquely identifying this selector.

- `elementTest`: A callback function to test whether an element should be included in the result set. If the function evaluates to `true` for an element, that element will be included in the resulting set; otherwise, the element will be excluded.

Description

Plug-ins can add selector expressions that allow scripts to find specific sets of DOM elements using a compact syntax. Generally, the expressions that plug-ins add are new pseudo-classes, identified by a leading : character.

The pseudo-classes that are supported by jQuery have the general format `:selectorName(param)`. Only the `selectorName` portion of this format is required; `param` is available if the pseudo-class allows parameters to make it more specific.

The element test callback receives the following four arguments, which it can use to determine whether the element passes the test:

- `element`: The DOM element under consideration. This is needed for most selectors.
- `index`: The index of the DOM element within the result set. This is helpful for selectors such as `:eq()` and `:lt()`.
- `matches`: An array containing the result of the regular expression that was used to parse this selector. Typically, `matches[3]` is the only relevant item in the array. In a selector of the `:selectorName(param)` form, the `matches[3]` item contains `param` — the text within the parentheses.
- `set`: The entire set of DOM elements matched up to this point. This parameter is rarely needed.

For example, we can build a pseudo-class that tests the number of elements that are child nodes of an element and call this new selector expression `:num-children(n)`:

```
jQuery.extend(jQuery.expr[':'], {
  'num-children': function(element, index, matches, set) {
    var count = 0;
    for (var node = element.firstChild; node; node =
                                        node.nextSibling) {
      if ( node.nodeType === 1 ) {
        count++;
      }
    }
    return count == matches[3];
  }
});
```

Now we can select all `<ul>` elements with exactly two child DOM elements, and turn them red:

```
$(document).ready(function() {
  $('ul:num-children(2)').css('color', 'red');
});
```

Plug-in conventions

Before sharing our plug-in with the world at `http://plugins.jquery.com/`, we should check to ensure that the code conforms to the following conventions.

Use of the $ alias

jQuery plug-ins may not assume that the `$` alias is available. Instead, the full jQuery name must be written out each time.

In longer plug-ins, many developers find that the lack of the $ shortcut makes code more difficult to read. To combat this, the shortcut can be locally defined for the scope of the plug-in by defining and executing a function. The syntax for defining and executing a function at once looks like this:

```
(function($) {
  // Code goes here
})(jQuery);
```

The wrapping function takes a single parameter to which we pass the global jQuery object. The parameter is named $. So within the function, we can use the $ alias with no conflicts.

Naming conventions

Plug-in files should be named jquery.myPlugin.js, where myPlugin is the name of our plug-in. This allows jQuery plug-ins to be easily distinguished from other JavaScript files.

Global functions within myPlugin should be named jQuery.myPlugin(), or should be grouped as methods of the jQuery.myPlugin object. This convention helps to guard against conflicts with other plug-ins.

API standardization

Methods defined by our plug-in must abide by the contract established by the jQuery API. In order to provide a consistent experience for plug-in users, these methods must observe the following rules:

- Methods should support implicit iteration
- Methods should preserve chaining unless otherwise explicitly documented
- Arguments to methods should provide reasonable and configurable defaults
- Method definitions must terminate with a semicolon (;) character to avoid errors during code compression

In addition to following these conventions, the API for the plug-in should be well-documented.

 Further details and related techniques can be found online, or in Chapter 11 of the book *Learning jQuery 1.3*.

11
Alphabetical Quick Reference

Having an entire chapter devoted to quick reference might seem redundant in a reference book. Still, it is quite a common experience to know the name of a function (or at least have a general idea of the function's name), but not know exactly what the function does. This alphabetical list is intended to help during those times when we need to quickly confirm a feature of the library and provide a pointer to the page where more detailed information is discussed.

Selector expressions

Modelled after the W3C's CSS 1-3 specification, jQuery's selector expressions are the primary means for finding elements on a page so that they can then be acted upon. All of the selectors in the following table are listed bare—not wrapped in the $() function—for easier and quicker browsing:

Expression	Description	Page
*	Select all elements	26
T	Select all elements that have a tag name of T	17
#myid	Select the unique element with an ID equal to myid	18
.myclass	Select all elements that have a class of myclass	18
[foo]	Select all elements that have the foo attribute with any value	27
[foo=bar]	Select all elements that have the foo attribute with a value exactly equal to bar	27
[foo!=bar]	Select all elements that do *not* have the foo attribute, or have a foo attribute but with a value other than bar	27

Expression	Description	Page
[foo^=bar]	Select all elements that have the foo attribute with a value *beginning* exactly with the string bar	28
[foo$=bar]	Select all elements that have the foo attribute with a value *ending* exactly with the string bar	28
[foo*=bar]	Select all elements that have the foo attribute with a value *containing* the substring bar	28
[foo~=bar]	Select all elements that have the foo attribute with a value containing the word bar, delimited by spaces	29
[foo|=bar]	Select all elements that have the foo attribute with a value either equal to bar, or beginning with bar and a hyphen (-).	29
E F	Select all elements matched by F that are descendants of an element matched by E	19
E > F	Select all elements matched by F that are children of an element matched by E	20
E + F	Select all elements matched by F that *immediately* follow and have the same parent as an element matched by E	20
E ~ F	Select all elements matched by F that follow and have the same parent as an element matched by E	21
E, F, G	Select all elements matched by any of the selector expressions E, F, or G	22
:animated	Select all elements that are in the progress of an animation at the time the selector is run	37
:button	Select all button elements and input elements with a type of button (<button>, <input type="button">)	30
:checkbox	Select all checkbox fields (<input type="checkbox">)	30
:checked	Select all form elements — checkboxes and radio buttons — that are checked	31
:contains(text)	Select all elements that contain the specified text	35
:disabled	Select all form elements that are disabled (that is, they have the disabled attribute and users cannot interact with them)	31
:empty	Select all elements that have no children (including text nodes)	25

Expression	Description	Page
`:enabled`	Select all form elements that are enabled (that is, they do not have the `disabled` attribute and users can interact with them)	30
`:eq(n)`	Select the element at index n within the matched set	31
`:even`	Select all elements with an even index within the matched set	33
`:file`	Select all file upload fields (`<input type="file">`)	30
`:first`	Select the first element within the matched set	32
`:first-child`	Select all elements that are the first child of their parent element	24
`:gt(n)`	Select all elements at an index greater than n within the matched set	32
`:has(E)`	Select all elements that contain an element matching E	35
`:header`	Select all elements that are headers, such as `<h1>` or `<h2>`	37
`:hidden`	Select all elements that are hidden	37
`:image`	Select all image inputs (`<input type="image">`)	30
`:input`	Select all form elements (`<input>` (all types), `<select>`, `<textarea>`, `<button>`)	30
`:last`	Select the last element within the matched set	33
`:last-child`	Select all elements that are the last child of their parent element	24
`:lt(n)`	Select all elements at an index less than n within the matched set	32
`:not(E)`	Select all elements that do not match the selector expression E	25
`:nth-child(n)` `:nth-child(even)` `:nth-child(odd)` `:nth-child(expr)`	Select all elements that are the nth child of their parent	22
`:odd`	Select all elements with an odd index within the matched set	34

Expression	Description	Page
`:only-child`	Select all elements that are the only child of their parent element	25
`:parent`	Select all elements that are the parent of another element, including text nodes	34
`:password`	Select all password fields (`<input type="password">`)	30
`:radio`	Select all radio button fields (`<input type="radio">`)	30
`:reset`	Select all reset buttons (`<input type="reset">`)	30
`:selected`	Select all form elements (effectively, `<option>` elements) that are currently selected	31
`:submit`	Select all submit inputs and button elements (`<input type="submit">`, `<button>`)	30
`:text`	Select all text fields (`<input type="text">`)	30
`:visible`	Select all elements that are visible	36

Methods

Every method in the jQuery library is listed in the following table. Methods that begin with a period (`.`) can be chained to a jQuery object created with `$()` or another method, and typically act on a set of DOM elements. Those that begin with `$.` are not chainable and typically act on a non-DOM object (such as the `XMLHttpRequest` object or a user-defined object).

Method	Description	Page
`.add(selector)` `.add(elements)` `.add(html)`	Add elements to the set of matched elements	68
`.addClass(className)` `.addClass(function)`	Add one or more classes to each element in the set of matched elements	92
`.after(content)` `.after(function)`	Insert content, specified by the parameter, after each element in the set of matched elements	114
`$.ajax(settings)`	Perform an asynchronous HTTP (AJAX) request	203
`.ajaxComplete(handler)`	Register a handler to be called when AJAX requests complete	215

Method	Description	Page
`.ajaxError(handler)`	Register a handler to be called when AJAX requests complete with an error	217
`.ajaxSend(handler)`	Register a handler to be called when AJAX requests are begun	218
`$.ajaxSetup(settings)`	Set default values for future AJAX requests	209
`.ajaxStart(handler)`	Register a handler to be called when the first AJAX request begins	219
`.ajaxStop(handler)`	Register a handler to be called when all AJAX requests have completed	220
`.ajaxSuccess(handler)`	Register a handler to be called when AJAX requests complete and are successful	221
`.andSelf()`	Add the previous set of elements on the stack to the current set	72
`.animate(properties[, duration][, easing][, callback])` `.animate(properties, options)`	Perform a custom animation of a set of CSS properties	193
`.append(content)` `.append(function)`	Insert content, specified by the parameter, at the end of each element in the set of matched elements	108
`.appendTo(target)`	Insert every element in the set of matched elements at the end of the target	109
`.attr(attributeName)`	Get the value of an attribute for the first element in the set of matched elements	77
`.attr(attributeName, value)` `.attr(map)` `.attr(attributeName, function)`	Set one or more attributes for the set of matched elements	78
`.before(content)` `.before(function)`	Insert content, specified by the parameter, before each element in the set of matched elements	111

Method	Description	Page
`.bind(eventType[, eventData], handler)`	Attach a handler to an event for the elements	127
`.blur(handler)` `.blur()`	Bind an event handler to the `blur` JavaScript event, or trigger that event on an element	163
`.change(handler)` `.change()`	Bind an event handler to the `change` JavaScript event, or trigger that event on an element	165
`.children([selector])`	Get the children of each element in the set of matched elements, optionally filtered by a selector	52
`.clearQueue([queueName])`	Remove from the queue all items that have not yet been executed	202
`.click(handler)` `.click()`	Bind an event handler to the `click` JavaScript event, or trigger that event on an element	148
`.clone([withEvents])`	Create a copy of the set of matched elements	121
`.closest(selector[, context])`	Get the first element that matches the selector, beginning at the current element and progressing up through the DOM tree	57
`.contents()`	Get the children of each element in the set of matched elements, including text nodes	74
`.css(propertyName)`	Get the value of a style property for the first element in the set of matched elements	80
`.css(propertyName, value)` `.css(map)` `.css(propertyName, function)`	Set one or more CSS properties for the set of matched elements	81
`.data(key, value)` `.data(obj)` `.data([key])`	Store or retrieve arbitrary data associated with the matched elements	246
`.dblclick(handler)` `.dblclick()`	Bind an event handler to the `dblclick` JavaScript event, or trigger that event on an element	149

Method	Description	Page
`.delay(duration[, queueName])`	Set a timer to delay execution of subsequent items on the queue for the matched elements	199
`.dequeue([queueName])`	Execute the next function on the queue for the matched elements	201
`.detach([selector])`	Remove the set of matched elements from the DOM	125
`.die(eventType[, handler])`	Remove an event handler previously attached using `.live()` from the elements	139
`.each(callback)` `$.each(collection, callback)`	Iterate over a collection, firing a callback function on each item	232
`.empty()`	Remove all child nodes of the set of matched elements from the DOM	122
`.end()`	End the most recent filtering operation in the current chain and return the set of matched elements to its previous state	70
`.error(handler)`	Bind an event handler to the `error` JavaScript event	144
`.eq(index)`	Reduce the set of matched elements to the one at the specified index	47
`$.extend([recursive, ] [target, ]properties[, propertiesN])`	Merge the contents of two objects together into the first object	240
`.fadeIn([duration] [, callback])`	Display the matched elements by fading them to opaque	189
`.fadeOut([duration] [, callback])`	Hide the matched elements by fading them to transparent	190
`.fadeTo(duration, opacity[, callback])`	Adjust the opacity of the matched elements	192
`.filter(selector)` `.filter(function)`	Reduce the set of matched elements to those that match the selector or pass the function's test	42

Method	Description	Page
`.find(selector)`	Get the descendants of each element in the current set of matched elements, filtered by a selector	51
`.first()`	Reduce the set of matched elements to the first one	48
`.focus(handler)` `.focus()`	Bind an event handler to the `focus` JavaScript event, or trigger that event on an element	162
`.focusin(handler)` `.focusin()`	Bind an event handler to the focusin JavaScript event, or trigger that event on an element	–
`.focusout(handler)` `.focusout()`	Bind an event handler to the focusout JavaScript event, or trigger that event on an element	–
`.get([index])`	Retrieve the DOM elements matched by the jQuery object	229
`$.get(url[, data][, success][, dataType])`	Load data from the server using a GET HTTP request	210
`$.getJSON(url[, data][, success])`	Load JSON-encoded data from the server using a GET HTTP request	213
`$.getScript(url[, success])`	Load JavaScript from the server using a GET HTTP request, and then execute it	214
`$.grep(array, filter[, invert])`	Winnow an array down to a selected set of items	234
`.has(selector)`	Reduce the set of matched elements to those that have an element matched by selector as a descendant	46
`.hasClass(className)`	Determine whether any of the matched elements are assigned the given class	92
`.height()`	Get the current computed height for the first element in the set of matched elements	82

Method	Description	Page
`.height(value)`	Set the CSS height of each element in the set of matched elements	83
`.hide([duration][, callback])`	Hide the matched elements	179
`.hover(handlerIn, handlerOut)`	Bind two handlers to the matched elements to be executed when the mouse pointer enters and leaves the elements	159
`.html()`	Get the HTML contents of the first element in the set of matched elements	97
`.html(htmlString)` `.html(function)`	Set the HTML contents of each element in the set of matched elements	97
`$.inArray(value, array)`	Search for a specified value within an array	236

`.index()`
`.index(element)`
`.index(string)`
	Search for a given element from among the matched elements	230

`.innerHeight()`	Get the current computed height for the first element in the set of matched elements, including padding but not border	84
`.innerWidth()`	Get the current computed width for the first element in the set of matched elements, including padding but not border	87
`.insertAfter(target)`	Insert every element in the set of matched elements after the target	115
`.insertBefore(target)`	Insert every element in the set of matched elements before the target	112
`.is(selector)`	Check the current matched set of elements against a selector and return true if at least one of these elements matches the selector	69

Method	Description	Page
`$.isArray(obj)`	Determine whether the argument is an array	244
`$.isEmptyObject(obj)`	Determine whether the argument is an empty JavaScript object	245
`$.isFunction(obj)`	Determine whether the argument is a function object	245
`$.isPlainObject(obj)`	Determine whether the argument is a plain JavaScript object	245
`.keydown(handler)` `.keydown()`	Bind an event handler to the `keydown` JavaScript event, or trigger that event on an element	169
`.keypress(handler)` `.keypress()`	Bind an event handler to the `keypress` JavaScript event, or trigger that event on an element	171
`.keyup(handler)` `.keyup()`	Bind an event handler to the `keyup` JavaScript event, or trigger that event on an element	172
`.last()`	Reduce the set of matched elements to the last one	49
`.live(eventType, handler)`	Attach a handler to the event for all elements that match the current selector, now or in the future	137
`.load(handler)`	Bind an event handler to the `load` JavaScript event	141
`.load(url[, data][, successs)`	Load data from the server and place the returned HTML into the matched element	211
`$.makeArray(obj)`	Convert an array-like object into a true JavaScript array	235
`.map(callback)`	Pass each item element in the current matched set through a function, producing a new jQuery object containing the return values	73
`$.map(array, transform)`	Transform an array into another one by using a transformation function	237

Method	Description	Page
`$.merge(array1, array2)`	Merge the contents of two arrays together into the first array	239
`.mousedown(handler)` `.mousedown()`	Bind an event handler to the mousedown JavaScript event, or trigger that event on an element	145
`.mouseenter(handler)` `.mouseenter()`	Bind an event handler to be fired when the mouse cursor enters an element, or trigger that handler on an element	156
`.mouseleave(handler)` `.mouseleave()`	Bind an event handler to be fired when the mouse cursor leaves an element, or trigger that handler on an element	157
`.mousemove(handler)` `.mousemove()`	Bind an event handler to the mousemove JavaScript event, or trigger that event on an element	160
`.mouseout(handler)` `.mouseout()`	Bind an event handler to the mouseout JavaScript event, or trigger that event on an element	154
`.mouseover(handler)` `.mouseover()`	Bind an event handler to the mouseover JavaScript event, or trigger that event on an element	152
`.mouseup(handler)` `.mouseup()`	Bind an event handler to the mouseup JavaScript event, or trigger that event on an element	146
`.next([selector])`	Get the immediately following sibling of each element in the set of matched elements, optionally filtered by a selector	64
`.nextAll([selector])`	Get all following siblings of each element in the set of matched elements, optionally filtered by a selector	65
`.nextUntil(selector)`	Get the next siblings of each element in the current set of matched elements up to but not including the element matched by the selector	66

Method	Description	Page
`$.noConflict([removeAll])`	Relinquish jQuery's control of the $ variable	227
`.not(selector)` `.not(elements)` `.not(function)`	Remove elements from the set of matched elements	44
`.offset()`	Get the current coordinates of the first element in the set of matched elements, relative to the document	88
`.offset(coordinates)`	Set the current coordinates of every element in the set of matched elements, relative to the document	89
`.offsetParent()`	Get the closest ancestor element that is positioned	59
`.one(eventType[, eventData], handler)`	Attach a handler to an event for the elements; the handler is executed at most once	134
`.outerHeight([includeMargin])`	Get the current computed height for the first element in the set of matched elements, including padding and border	84
`.outerWidth([includeMargin])`	Get the current computed width for the first element in the set of matched elements, including padding and border	87
`$.param(obj[, traditional])`	Create a serialized representation of an object or array, suitable for use in a URL query string or AJAX request.	243
`.parent([selector])`	Get the parent of each element in the current set of matched elements, optionally filtered by a selector	56
`.parents([selector])`	Get the ancestors of each element in the current set of matched elements, optionally filtered by a selector	53

Method	Description	Page
`.parentsUntil(selector)`	Get the ancestors of each element in the current set of matched elements up to but not including the element matched by the selector	55
`.position()`	Get the current coordinates of the first element in the set of matched elements, relative to the offset parent	89
`$.post(url[, data][, success][, dataType])`	Load data from the server using a POST HTTP request	212
`.prepend(content)` `.prepend(function)`	Insert content, specified by the parameter, at the beginning of each element in the set of matched elements	104
`.prependTo(target)`	Insert every element in the set of matched elements at the beginning of the target	106
`.prev([selector])`	Get the immediately preceding sibling of each element in the set of matched elements, optionally filtered by a selector	61
`.prevAll([selector])`	Get all preceding siblings of each element in the set of matched elements, optionally filtered by a selector	62
`.prevUntil(selector)`	Get the previous siblings of each element in the current set of matched elements up to but not including the element matched by the selector	63
`.queue([queueName])` `.queue([queueName], newQueue)` `.queue([queueName], callback)`	Manipulate the queue of functions to be executed on the matched elements	200
`$(document).ready(handler)` `$().ready(handler)` `$(handler)`	Specify a function to execute when the DOM is fully loaded	140
`.remove([selector])`	Remove the set of matched elements from the DOM	123

Method	Description	Page
`.removeAttr(attributeName)` `.removeAttr(function)`	Remove an attribute from each element in the set of matched elements	80
`.removeClass([className])` `.removeClass([function])`	Remove one or all classes from each element in the set of matched elements	93
`.removeData([key])`	Remove a previously stored piece of data	248
`.replaceAll(target)`	Replace each target element with the set of matched elements	103
`.replaceWith(newContent)`	Replace each element in the set of matched elements with the provided new content	102
`.resize(handler)` `.resize()`	Bind an event handler to the `resize` JavaScript event, or trigger that event on an element	174
`.scroll(handler)` `.scroll()`	Bind an event handler to the `scroll` JavaScript event, or trigger that event on an element	175
`.scrollLeft()`	Get the current horizontal position of the scroll bar for the first element in the set of matched elements	91
`.scrollLeft(value)`	Set the current horizontal position of the scroll bar for each of the set of matched elements	91
`.scrollTop()`	Get the current vertical position of the scroll bar for the first element in the set of matched elements	90
`.scrollTop(value)`	Set the current vertical position of the scroll bar for each of the set of matched elements	90
`.select(handler)` `.select()`	Bind an event handler to the `select` JavaScript event, or trigger that event on an element	166
`.serialize()`	Encode a set of form elements as a string for submission	223
`.serializeArray()`	Encode a set of form elements as an array of names and values	224

Method	Description	Page
`.show([duration] [, callback])`	Display the matched elements	177
`.siblings([selector])`	Get the siblings of each element in the set of matched elements, optionally filtered by a selector	60
`.size()`	Return the number of DOM elements matched by the jQuery object	228
`.slice(start [, end])`	Reduce the set of matched elements to a subset specified by a range of indices	49
`.slideDown([duration] [, callback])`	Display the matched elements with a sliding motion	184
`.slideToggle([duration] [, callback])`	Display or hide the matched elements with a sliding motion	186
`.slideUp([duration] [, callback])`	Hide the matched elements with a sliding motion	185
`.stop([clearQueue] [, jumpToEnd])`	Stop the currently-running animation on the matched elements	198
`.submit(handler)` `.submit()`	Bind an event handler to the `submit` JavaScript event, or trigger that event on an element	167
`.text()`	Get the combined text contents of each element in the set of matched elements, including their descendants	98
`.text(textString)` `.text(function)`	Set the content of each element in the set of matched elements to the specified text	99
`.toArray()`	Convert an array-like object (such as the jQuery object) to a true array	–
`.toggle([duration] [, callback])` `.toggle(showOrHide)`	Display or hide the matched elements	181
`.toggle(handlerEven, handlerOdd [, additionalHandlers...])`	Bind two or more handlers to the matched elements to be executed on alternate clicks	151

Method	Description	Page
`.toggleClass(className)` `.toggleClass(className, addOrRemove)` `.toggleClass(function[, addOrRemove])`	If the class is present, remove it from each element in the set of matched elements; if it is not present, add the class	95
`.trigger(eventType[, extraParameters])`	Execute all handlers and behaviors attached to the matched elements for the given event type	135
`.triggerHandler(eventType[, extraParameters])`	Execute all handlers attached to an element for an event	136
`$.trim(string)`	Remove whitespace from the ends of a string	242
`.unbind([eventType[, handler]])` `.unbind(event)`	Remove a previously-attached event handler from the elements	131
`$.unique(array)`	Create a copy of an array of DOM elements with the duplicates removed	240
`.unload(handler)`	Bind an event handler to the `unload` JavaScript event	143
`.unwrap()`	Remove a containing element while keeping its contents	125
`.val()`	Get the current value of the first element in the set of matched elements	101
`.val(value)` `.val(function)`	Set the value of each element in the set of matched elements	101
`.width()`	Get the current computed width for the first element in the set of matched elements	85
`.width(value)`	Set the CSS width of each element in the set of matched elements	86

Method	Description	Page
`.wrap(wrappingElement)` `.wrap(wrappingFunction)`	Wrap an HTML structure around each element in the set of matched elements	117
`.wrapAll(wrappingElement)`	Wrap an HTML structure around all elements in the set of matched elements	118
`.wrapInner(wrappingElement)` `.wrapInner(wrappingFunction)`	Wrap an HTML structure around the content of each element in the set of matched elements	119

Properties

The following properties are available for inspecting both the browser environment and individual jQuery objects.

Property	Description	Page
`$.browser`	Information about the user agent displaying the page	249
`.context`	The DOM context that was used to create the jQuery object	254
`.length`	The number of DOM elements matched by the jQuery object	252
`.selector`	The selector string that was used to create the jQuery object	253
`$.support`	Information about the browser's support for specific rendering and JavaScript features	250

Online Resources

The following online resources represent a starting point for learning more about jQuery, JavaScript, and web development in general beyond what is covered in this book. There are far too many sources of quality information on the Web for this appendix to approach anything resembling an exhaustive list. Furthermore, while other print publications can also provide valuable information, they are not noted here.

jQuery documentation

These resources offer references and details on the jQuery library itself.

Official jQuery documentation

The documentation on `jquery.com` includes the full jQuery API, tutorials, getting started guides, and more: `http://docs.jquery.com/`.

jQuery API browser

In addition to the HTML version at `docs.jquery.com`, the API is available via a convenient browser application: `http://api.jquery.com/`.

Adobe AIR jQuery API Viewer

Remy Sharp has packaged the jQuery API into an Adobe AIR application for offline viewing. A Flash AIR installer available at `http://api.jquery.com/` is the recommended method of installing the viewer. It is also available for direct download at the following address: `http://remysharp.com/downloads/jquery-api-browser.air.zip`.

JavaScript reference

These sites offer references and guides to JavaScript as a language in general, rather than jQuery in particular.

Mozilla Developer Center

This site has a comprehensive JavaScript reference, a guide to programming with JavaScript, links to helpful tools, and more: `http://developer.mozilla.org/en/docs/JavaScript/`.

Client-Side JavaScript Reference

This online book provided by Sun is "a reference manual for the JavaScript language, including both core and client-side JavaScript for version 1.3": `http://docs.sun.com/source/816-6408-10/contents.htm`.

MSDN Reference

The **Microsoft Developer Network (MSDN)** JScript Reference provides descriptions of the full set of functions, objects, and so on. It's especially helpful for understanding Microsoft's implementation of the ECMAScript standard in Internet Explorer: `http://msdn.microsoft.com/en-us/library/x85xxsf4(VS.71).aspx`.

Additionally, the MSDN, HTML, and DHTML reference provides descriptions of collections, events, constants, methods, objects, and properties in the DHTML Object Model. As with the JScript Reference, it can be especially useful for cases in which Internet Explorer deviates from the standard or Internet Explorer's interpretation of an ambiguous specification differs from that of other major browsers: `http://msdn.microsoft.com/en-us/library/ms533050%28VS.85%29.aspx`.

Dev.Opera

While focused primarily on its own browser platform, Opera's site for web developers includes a number of useful articles on JavaScript: `http://dev.opera.com/articles/`.

Quirksmode

Peter-Paul Koch's Quirksmode site is a terrific resource for understanding differences in the way browsers implement various JavaScript functions, as well as many CSS properties: `http://www.quirksmode.org/`.

JavaScript Toolbox

Matt Kruse's JavaScript Toolbox offers a large assortment of homespun JavaScript libraries, as well as sound advice on JavaScript best practices and a collection of vetted JavaScript resources elsewhere on the Web: http://www.javascripttoolbox.com/.

comp.lang.javascript FAQ

This page includes a very lengthy list of questions frequently asked on the *comp.lang.javascript* Usenet group, along with answers and links to further information: http://www.jibbering.com/faq/.

JavaScript code compressors

When putting the finishing touches on a site, it is often advisable to minify the JavaScript code. This process reduces download time for all users of the site, especially when coupled with server-side compression.

JSMin

Created by *Douglas Crockford*, JSMin is a filter that removes comments and unnecessary whitespaces from JavaScript files. It typically reduces file size by half, resulting in faster downloads, especially when combined with server-based file compression. Some web sites host the tool to allow users to minify their code by pasting it into a textarea. JSMin can be downloaded as an MS-DOS .exe file or as source code written in a variety of programming languages: http://www.crockford.com/javascript/jsmin.html.

YUI Compressor

The YUI Compressor is "designed to be 100% safe and yield a higher compression ratio than most other tools". As of version 2.0, it is also able to minify CSS files. It requires Java version 1.4 or greater: http://developer.yahoo.com/yui/compressor/.

Google Closure Compiler

This new service from Google performs a similar compression to JSMin, and in some tests has been found to achieve a higher degree of compression. The compiler is available as both a standalone application and an on-demand API.

This tool also integrates a JavaScript syntax checker that warns of possible errors and code defects: http://code.google.com/closure/compiler/.

Packer

This JavaScript compressor/obfuscator by *Dean Edwards* was used to compress the source code of previous versions of jQuery. The tool is available as a web-based tool or as a free download. The resulting code is very efficient in file size at a cost of a small increase in execution time. Although it is no longer officially recommended, it may be a legitimate option when server-side file compression is not available:

```
http://dean.edwards.name/packer/
```

```
http://dean.edwards.name/download/#packer
```

JavaScript code decompressors

It may be necessary at times to reverse the results of minification or compression/obfuscation in order to debug or learn from the code. The following online tools can help.

Pretty Printer

This tool prettifies JavaScript that has been compressed, restoring line breaks and indentation where possible. It provides a number of options for tailoring the results: `http://www.prettyprinter.de/`.

JavaScript beautifier

Similar to Pretty Printer, this tool unpacks compressed or minified code to make it much more readable. In addition to the web-based version, the JavaScript beautifier is available as a command-line tool using the Rhino JavaScript engine and as an add-on to the Fiddler web debugging proxy for Windows: `http://jsbeautifier.org/`.

(X)HTML reference

The jQuery library is at its best when working with properly formatted semantic HTML and XHTML documents. The resource below provides assistance with these markup languages.

W3C Hypertext Markup Language Home Page

The **World Wide Web Consortium** (**W3C**) sets the standard for (X)HTML, and the HTML home page is a great launching point for its specifications and guidelines: `http://www.w3.org/MarkUp/`.

Additionally, the new HTML5 Editor's Draft contains information about the upcoming version of the HTML specification: `http://dev.w3.org/html5/spec/Overview.html`.

CSS reference

The effects and animations we have seen time and again all rely on the power of Cascading Stylesheets. To incorporate the visual flourishes we desire in our sites, we may need to turn to these CSS resources for guidance.

W3C Cascading Style Sheets Home Page

The W3C's CSS home page provides links to tutorials, specifications, test suites, and other resources: `http://www.w3.org/Style/CSS/`.

Mezzoblue CSS Crib Sheet

Dave Shea provides this helpful CSS Crib Sheet in an attempt to make the design process easier, and provides a quick reference to check when you run into trouble: `http://mezzoblue.com/css/cribsheet/`.

Position Is Everything

This site includes a catalog of CSS browser bugs along with explanations of how to overcome them: `http://www.positioniseverything.net/`.

Useful blogs

New techniques and features are always being developed and introduced for any living technology. Staying on top of innovations can be made easier by checking in with these sources of web development news from time to time.

The jQuery blog

John Resig and other contributors to the official jQuery blog post announcements about new versions and other initiatives among the project team, as well as occasional tutorials and editorial pieces: `http://blog.jquery.com/`.

Learning jQuery

Karl Swedberg runs this blog for jQuery tutorials, techniques, and announcements. Guest authors include jQuery team members *Mike Alsup* and *Brandon Aaron*: `http://www.learningjquery.com/`.

jQuery for Designers

This blog by *Remy Sharp* offers a number of tutorials and screencasts aimed primarily at designers who want to leverage the power of jQuery: `http://jqueryfordesigners.com/`.

Ajaxian

This frequently-updated blog begun by *Dion Almaer* and *Ben Galbraith* provides a tremendous amount of news and features and the occasional tutorial about JavaScript: `http://ajaxian.com/`.

John Resig

The creator of jQuery, *John Resig*, discusses advanced JavaScript topics on his personal blog: `http://ejohn.org/`.

JavaScript Ant

This site contains a repository of articles pertaining to JavaScript and its usage in modern web browsers, as well as an organized list of JavaScript resources found elsewhere on the Web: `http://javascriptant.com/`.

Robert's talk

Robert Nyman writes about developing for the Internet, especially client-side scripting: `http://www.robertnyman.com/`.

Snook

Jonathan Snook's general programming/web-development blog has a number of useful articles on advanced JavaScript and CSS techniques: `http://snook.ca/`.

Paul Irish

Paul Irish writes about jQuery, JavaScript, and cutting-edge web development topics: `http://paulirish.com/`.

NCZOnline

The blog of *Nicholas C. Zakas* contains reviews and articles on web site performance, JavaScript, and other web-related topics: `http://www.nczonline.net/blog/`.

I Can't

Three sites by *Christian Heilmann* provide blog entries, sample code, and lengthy articles related to JavaScript and web development:

`http://icant.co.uk/`

`http://www.wait-till-i.com/`

`http://www.onlinetools.org/`

DOM scripting

Jeremy Keith's blog picks up where the popular DOM scripting book leaves off—a fantastic resource for unobtrusive JavaScript: `http://domscripting.com/blog/`.

Steve Souders

Author of the acclaimed books *High Performance Websites* and *Even Faster Websites* Steve Souders posts the results of his research on performance-related issues on his web site: `http://www.stevesouders.com/blog/`.

As days pass by

Stuart Langridge experiments with advanced use of the browser DOM: `http://www.kryogenix.org/code/browser/`.

A List Apart

A List Apart explores the design, development, and meaning of web content with a special focus on web standards and best practices: `http://www.alistapart.com/`.

Web development frameworks using jQuery

As developers of open source projects become aware of jQuery, many are incorporating the JavaScript library into their own systems. The following is an abbreviated list of these adopters:

CouchDB: `http://couchdb.apache.org/`

Digitalus CMS: `http://code.google.com/p/digitalus-cms/`

DotNetNuke: `http://www.dotnetnuke.com/`

Drupal: `http://drupal.org/`

DutchPIPE: `http://dutchpipe.org/`

ExpressionEngine: `http://expressionengine.com/`

Hpricot: `http://wiki.github.com/hpricot/hpricot`

JobberBase: `http://www.jobberbase.com/`

Laconica: `http://laconi.ca/`

Piwik: `http://piwik.org/`

Plone: `http://plone.org`

Pommo: `http://pommo.org/`

simfony: `http://www.symfony-project.org/`

SPIP: `http://www.spip.net/`

Textpattern: `http://www.textpattern.com/`

Trac: `http://trac.edgewall.org/`

WordPress: `http://wordpress.org/`

Z-Blog: `http://www.rainbowsoft.org/zblog`

For a more complete list, visit the *Sites Using jQuery* page at: `http://docs.jquery.com/Sites_Using_jQuery`.

B
Development Tools

Documentation can help in troubleshooting issues with our JavaScript applications, but there is no replacement for a good set of software development tools. Fortunately, there are many software packages available for inspecting and debugging JavaScript code, and most of them are available for free.

Tools for Firefox

Mozilla Firefox is the browser of choice for the lion's share of web developers and, therefore, has some of the most extensive and well-respected development tools.

Firebug

The Firebug extension for Firefox is indispensable for jQuery development: `http://www.getfirebug.com/`.

Some of the features of Firebug are:

- An excellent DOM inspector for finding names and selectors for pieces of the document
- CSS manipulation tools for finding out why a page looks a certain way and changing it
- An interactive JavaScript console
- A JavaScript debugger that can watch variables and trace code execution

Firebug has spawned a number of its own extensions, which make the tool even more versatile. A few of the more popular Firebug extensions are:

- **YSlow**: For page-load performance testing:
  `http://developer.yahoo.com/yslow/`
- **FireUnit**: For simple test logging and viewing within a Firebug tab:
  `http://fireunit.org/`
- **FireCookie**: For viewing and managing cookies within a Firebug tab:
  `http://code.google.com/p/firecookie/`

Web Developer toolbar

This not only overlaps Firebug in the area of DOM inspection, but also contains tools for common tasks such as cookie manipulation, form inspection, and page resizing. You can also use this toolbar to quickly and easily disable JavaScript for a site to ensure that functionality degrades gracefully when the user's browser is less capable: `http://chrispederick.com/work/web-developer/`.

Venkman

Venkman is the official JavaScript debugger for the Mozilla project. It provides a troubleshooting environment that is reminiscent of the GDB system for debugging programs that are written in other languages: `http://www.mozilla.org/projects/venkman/`.

Regular Expressions Tester

Regular expressions for matching strings in JavaScript can be tricky to craft. This extension for Firefox allows easy experimentation with regular expressions using an interface for entering search text: `http://sebastianzartner.ath.cx/new/downloads/RExT/`.

Tools for Internet Explorer

Sites often behave differently in IE than in other web browsers, so having debugging tools for this platform is important.

Microsoft Internet Explorer Developer Toolbar

The Developer Toolbar for Internet Explorer versions 6 and 7 primarily provides a view of the DOM tree for a web page. Elements can be located visually and modified on the fly with new CSS rules. It also provides other miscellaneous development aids, such as a ruler for measuring page elements: `http://www.microsoft.com/downloads/details.aspx?FamilyID=e59c3964-672d-4511-bb3e-2d5e1db91038`.

Microsoft Internet Explorer 8 Developer Tools

Internet Explorer 8 comes with a set of developer tools that is much improved over previous versions' Developer Toolbar. Somewhat resembling Firefox's Firebug extension, the Developer Tools suite provides a console for JavaScript execution and logging, as well as tabs for JavaScript debugging and profiling, and CSS and HTML inspection and modification.

Microsoft Visual Web Developer Express

Microsoft's free Visual Web Developer Express package can be used not only to build web pages, but also to inspect and debug JavaScript code: `http://www.microsoft.com/express/vwd/`.

To run the debugger interactively, follow the process outlined here: `http://www.berniecode.com/blog/2007/03/08/how-to-debug-javascript-with-visual-web-developer-express/`.

dynaTrace AJAX Edition

This free tool gathers an enormous amount of performance data for web applications and displays it in a number of ways for further analysis: `http://ajax.dynatrace.com/pages/`.

DebugBar

The DebugBar provides a DOM inspector as well as a JavaScript console for debugging. It is especially useful for Internet Explorer 6 and 7, which do not have their own consoles: `http://www.debugbar.com/`.

Drip

Memory leaks in JavaScript code can cause performance and stability issues for Internet Explorer. Drip helps to detect and isolate these memory issues: `http://Sourceforge.net/projects/ieleak/`.

Tools for Safari

Safari's suite of developer tools has come a long way since its inception.

Develop menu

As of Safari 3.1, an option in **Preferences | Advanced** provides a special menu called **Develop**. With this menu enabled, the following developer tools are available:

- **Web Inspector**: Inspect individual page elements and collect information especially about the CSS rules that apply to each one
- **Error Console**: Not just for logging errors, this console is similar to the console in Firebug and Internet Explorer 8's Developer Tools
- JavaScript debugging and profiling
- Resource tracking
- Disabling browser features such as caches, images, styles, and JavaScript

Tools for Opera

While it has a limited market share as a desktop browser, Opera is a significant player in embedded systems and mobile devices, and its capabilities should be considered during web development.

Dragonfly

While still in its early stages, Dragonfly is a promising debugging environment for Opera browsers on computers or mobile devices. Dragonfly's feature set is similar to that of Firebug, including JavaScript debugging as well as CSS and DOM inspection and editing: `http://www.opera.com/dragonfly/`.

Other tools

While the previous tools each focus on a specific browser, these utilities are broader in their scope.

Firebug Lite

Though the Firebug extension itself is limited to the Firefox web browser, some of the features can be replicated by including the Firebug Lite script on the web page. This package simulates the Firebug console, including allowing calls to `console.log()` to work in all browsers and not raise JavaScript errors: `http://www.getfirebug.com/lite.html`.

NitobiBug

Like Firebug Lite, NotobiBug is a cross-browser tool that covers some of the same ground as the more robust and refined Firebug. Its strength lies in its DOM and object inspection, though it has a capable console as well. The console and inspector can be invoked by including a reference to the Nitobi JavaScript file and calling `nitobi.Debug.log()`: `http://www.nitobibug.com/`.

TextMate jQuery Bundle

This extension for the popular Mac OS X text editor TextMate provides syntax highlighting for jQuery methods and selectors, code completion for methods, and a quick API reference from within your code. The bundle is also compatible with the E text editor for Windows: `http://github.com/kswedberg/jquery-tmbundle/`.

jQuerify Bookmarklet

This bookmarklet runs jQuery on web pages that don't already have it loaded, which allows us to experiment with jQuery on those sites in a console such as the one provided by Firebug or Safari's Develop menu: `http://www.learningjquery.com/2009/04/better-stronger-safer-jquerify-bookmarklet`.

Charles

When developing AJAX-intensive applications, it can be useful to see exactly what data is being sent between the browser and the server. The Charles web debugging proxy displays all HTTP traffic between two points, including normal web requests, HTTPS traffic, Flash remoting, and AJAX responses: `http://www.charlesproxy.com/`.

Fiddler

Fiddler is another useful HTTP debugging proxy with features similar to those in Charles. According to its site, Fiddler "includes a powerful event-based scripting subsystem, and can be extended using any .NET language": `http://www.fiddler2.com/fiddler2/`.

Sloppy

Sloppy is a Java-based web proxy that, according to its web site, "deliberately slows the transfer of data between client and server" in order to simulate loading web pages with a dial-up connection at various bandwidths: `http://www.dallaway.com/sloppy/`.

JS Bin

JS Bin is a collaborative JavaScript Debugging tool for rapid prototyping and sharing of scripts. It has a three-tab interface for writing JavaScript and HTML and viewing the output, and it automatically loads one of a handful of JavaScript libraries via a select list: `http://jsbin.com/`.

Bespin

Bespin is a web-based, extensible code editor with collaboration features. It allows users to create an entire web site on Bespin's server and then deploy it to another server. As it uses the HTML5 Canvas element for rendering the code, only the most recent versions of Firefox, Safari, or Chrome are supported: `https://bespin.mozilla.com/`.

Aptana

This Java-based web development IDE is free and cross-platform. Along with both standard and advanced code-editing features, it incorporates a full copy of the jQuery API documentation and has its own Firebug-based JavaScript debugger: `http://www.aptana.com/`.

Index

Symbols

PACKT PUBLISHING

Thank you for buying
jQuery 1.4 Reference Guide

Packt Open Source Project Royalties

When we sell a book written on an Open Source project, we pay a royalty directly to that project. Therefore by purchasing jQuery 1.4 Reference Guide, Packt will have given some of the money received to the jQuery project.

In the long term, we see ourselves and you—customers and readers of our books—as part of the Open Source ecosystem, providing sustainable revenue for the projects we publish on. Our aim at Packt is to establish publishing royalties as an essential part of the service and support a business model that sustains Open Source.

If you're working with an Open Source project that you would like us to publish on, and subsequently pay royalties to, please get in touch with us.

Writing for Packt

We welcome all inquiries from people who are interested in authoring. Book proposals should be sent to author@packtpub.com. If your book idea is still at an early stage and you would like to discuss it first before writing a formal book proposal, contact us; one of our commissioning editors will get in touch with you.

We're not just looking for published authors; if you have strong technical skills but no writing experience, our experienced editors can help you develop a writing career, or simply get some additional reward for your expertise.

About Packt Publishing

Packt, pronounced 'packed', published its first book "Mastering phpMyAdmin for Effective MySQL Management" in April 2004 and subsequently continued to specialize in publishing highly focused books on specific technologies and solutions.

Our books and publications share the experiences of your fellow IT professionals in adapting and customizing today's systems, applications, and frameworks. Our solution-based books give you the knowledge and power to customize the software and technologies you're using to get the job done. Packt books are more specific and less general than the IT books you have seen in the past. Our unique business model allows us to bring you more focused information, giving you more of what you need to know, and less of what you don't.

Packt is a modern, yet unique publishing company, which focuses on producing quality, cutting-edge books for communities of developers, administrators, and newbies alike. For more information, please visit our website: www.PacktPub.com.

Learning jQuery 1.3

ISBN: 978-1-847196-70-5   Paperback: 444 pages

Better Interaction Design and Web Development with Simple JavaScript Techniques

1. An introduction to jQuery that requires minimal programming experience

2. Detailed solutions to specific client-side problems

3. For web designers to create interactive elements for their designs

jQuery 1.3 with PHP

ISBN: 978-1-847196-98-9   Paperback: 248 pages

Enhance your PHP applications by increasing their responsiveness through jQuery and its plugins.

1. Combine client-side jQuery with your server-side PHP to make your applications more efficient and exciting for the client

2. Learn about some of the most popular jQuery plugins and methods

3. Create powerful and responsive user interfaces for your PHP applications

Please check **www.PacktPub.com** for information on our titles

Breinigsville, PA USA
15 February 2010
232517BV00001B/3/P